PRACTICAL FISHKEEPING

PRACTICAL FISHKEEPING

THE ULTIMATE GUIDE TO SETTING UP AND MAINTAINING FRESHWATER, BRACKISH AND MARINE FISH TANKS

MARY BAILEY &
GINA SANDFORD

Select Editions imprint specially produced for Selectabook Ltd

Produced by Anness Publishing Limited
Hermes House, 88-89 Blackfriars Road, London SE1 8HA

A CIP catalogue record for this book is available from the British Library

ISBN 1 84 081 087 4

Printed and bound in Singapore

1 3 5 7 9 10 8 6 4 2

Half title pages: Astronotus ocellatus **(oscar)**
Title page: Poecilia reticulata **(guppy)**
Above: Phractocephalus hemioliopterus **(red tailed catfish)**
Opposite, from top: Botia macracantha **(clown loach),** ***Amphiprion rubrocinctus*** **(Fijian clown),**
Microgeophagus ramirezi **(ram cichlid)**

Contents

Introduction

You have decided to become a fishkeeper, or you are at least thinking about it. You may have been impressed by an aquarium you have seen recently, or perhaps you are looking for an interesting spare-time activity. You may not realize it, but you are standing at a crossroads! Ahead of you lies not just a new hobby, but, provided you take the right path, a lifetime of enjoyment and a host of new friends. The other roads, however, lead to disillusionment and disaster, and yet another "aquarium for sale" advertisement in the local paper.

This book aims to point you in the right direction, and to ensure that you stay on the straight and narrow thereafter. Our unique hands-on approach tells you not only what to do, but also what to avoid. Between us we have more years of fishkeeping experience than we care to remember, during which, like all aquarists, we have learnt from our mistakes; and, as "aquatic agony aunts", we have come across most of the other likely (and unlikely!) pitfalls and problems. We hope to help you avoid them. You may find us sometimes blunter than other authors, but that is because there must be no misunderstandings where lives are at stake.

The key to success is always to know what you are doing *before* you start doing it. That may sound obvious, but it is astonishing how many people think fishkeeping is just a matter of filling an aquarium with water and adding fishes. Everyone knows that water can be hard or soft, so why assume all fishes will thrive in what comes out of a particular tap? And hardness is just one of the parameters to be considered. From the fishes' viewpoint it is irrelevant that you are only a beginner – if you don't get it right then they will be at best stressed, at worst dead. The moment you acquire a fish you become responsible for its welfare, hence our golden rule: no matter how expert you become, *always do your homework first*. We cannot hope to tell you everything you will ever need to know, nor can we guarantee success – that still depends on you – but we will guide you through the basic principles of aquarium management.

We will discuss the role the aquarist can – and should – play in conservation, a topic which nowadays is increasingly important in our hobby. New species help to stimulate continued interest and fresh blood is needed to strengthen captive breeding lines, but over-exploitation of wild stock must be avoided. It is essential that every aquarist shows a responsible attitude, taking the best possible care of his or her fishes, and making every attempt to breed them.

As your experience increases, you will realize that your new hobby can, if you choose, involve far more than a living-room ornament or casual pastime. You may become a botanist, entomologist, geologist, handyman – the list is almost endless. No matter in which directions your interests lead you, we hope this book will be your guiding light.

Right: **Take as much care when buying your plants as when purchasing your fishes, and avoid specimens that have dead and dying foliage.**

Getting Started

It is easy to decide that owning an aquarium would be a nice idea, but it can be difficult to know just where and how to start. We have already introduced you to the concept of "homework", and in the first instance this means making sure you know exactly what is involved before you acquire any equipment, let alone fishes. You are already on the right track in that you are reading this book before making any purchases, and we would urge you to finish it before going any further, as you will then be in a better position to make various basic decisions – including whether you want to be a fishkeeper after all! If, as we hope you will, you decide to go ahead, you can then re-read this book, using it as a step-by-step guide to planning, setting up, and running your first aquarium.

Having done your preliminary homework, you must ask yourself a number of basic questions: What size aquarium can I accommodate (and afford)? What sort of fishes would I like to keep? Small or large (aquarium size permitting)? Freshwater or marine? Coldwater or tropical? What are their specific requirements and habits? Will they live in my tap water and, if not, am I prepared to go to the trouble and expense of providing the right conditions? Will they get along with each other? Do I want to grow plants? Will my preferred fishes eat them? Life being what it is, you may have to compromise when it comes to your personal inclinations, but *never* do so when it comes to the fishes' welfare. That must *always* come first.

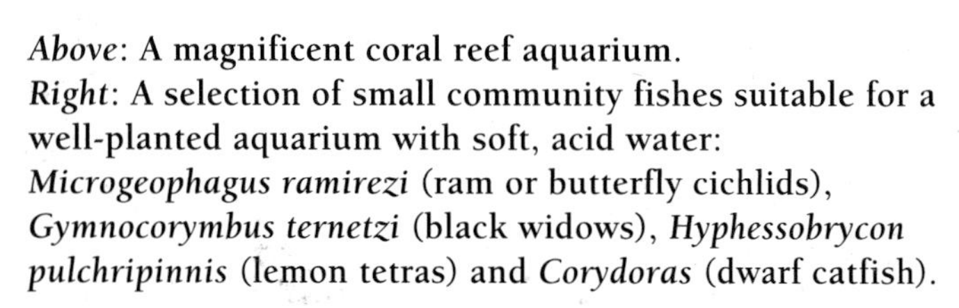

Above: A magnificent coral reef aquarium.
Right: A selection of small community fishes suitable for a well-planted aquarium with soft, acid water: *Microgeophagus ramirezi* (ram or butterfly cichlids), *Gymnocorymbus ternetzi* (black widows), *Hyphessobrycon pulchripinnis* (lemon tetras) and *Corydoras* (dwarf catfish).

Deciding What Kinds of Fishes To Keep

Although considerations of expense and the space you have available may limit your options, do, if possible, let your preferred choice of fishes dictate factors such as aquarium size rather than *vice versa*, as keeping the species you really want is bound to increase your motivation and enjoyment. Establishing your preferences will require a certain amount of effort in finding out what species are available, making a list of those you find attractive, and applying the above questions to them. You are bound to find that some are incompatible with available space, each other, and your personal concept of a miniature underwater paradise, but the wide choice available should enable you to compile a suitable shortlist without undue trouble.

In deciding what fishes to keep you must consider how many your aquarium can accommodate. This is often calculated in terms of oxygen requirement, based on centimetres of fish (length excluding the tail when full-grown) relative to the surface area of the tank: for freshwater fishes 2.5 cm of fish per 194 cm^2 (1 inch per 30 square inches) of surface (coldwater) or 2.5 cm per 64 cm^2 (1 inch per 10 square inches) (tropical). For marines the formula is 2.5 cm of fish per 18 litres (1 inch per 4 gallons) for the first 6 months, then 2.5 cm per 9 litres (1 inch per 2 gallons). For some fishes, however, population density may be governed by territorial requirements, and fewer fishes can be kept than is suggested by the above formulae.

Fish Compatibility

The compatibility (or otherwise) of fish species must always be taken into consideration before they are mixed. First of all, environmental requirements must be similar. Mercifully, few people try to mix marine and freshwater species, but many attempt (unsuccessfully) to keep brackish water fishes in freshwater aquaria. Even more fail to realize the varying degrees of hardness and acidity/alkalinity occurring in different freshwater biotopes, and that fishes from these different water chemistries do best if given natural conditions in captivity. Temperature requirements should also be similar. Some fishes come from fast-flowing streams, others from still pools, and the needs of both cannot be satisfied in one aquarium. Some prefer rocky habitats, others jungles of plants, yet others open space; some require bright light, some require dim. All these points must be considered when evaluating their environmental compatibility.

Carassius auratus (the goldfish) is a coldwater fish which can be kept in an aquarium or pond, but should never be confined to a bowl or other small container.

Monodactylus argenteus (the mono) requires a good-sized brackish water tropical aquarium.

Corydoras catfishes, by contrast, will not tolerate salt.

When selecting fishes, avoid poorly coloured specimens such as these *Phenacogrammus interruptus* (Congo tetras) as this is often the first signs of stress due to poor or wrong water conditioning.

There are several interesting North American cold water fishes available such as this *Phoxinus erythrogaster*.

Lake Malawi mouthbrooding cichlids such as this *Melanochromis chipokae* require very specific conditions.

***Pterois volitans* (the lion or dragon fish) is a lurking predator of the coral reef, and may eat small tankmates.**

***Thorichthys meeki* (the firemouth) is often sold as a community fish, but is quite unsuitable. It grows to 10 cm (4 in), is territorial, and may eat smaller tankmates.**

Size and Temperament

Size and temperament are just as important. Although not all species feed exclusively on other fishes, it is natural for larger fishes to eat smaller ones. So, except where dealing only with strict vegetarians, always ensure the smallest fish is too big to fit into the largest mouth – and that, allowing for future growth, it will remain so. Some fishes are territorial, occupying an area which usually represents either their private larder or their intended nursery (feeding and breeding territory respectively). They are usually aggressive towards conspecifics (members of their own species) in particular, and frequently towards other species as well. They can sometimes be kept with other fishes if the latter are evenly matched (in size and temperament), but they may need their own tank.

Think about feeding. Do you really want to keep fishes with varying specialized dietary needs, requiring you to serve a variety of foods at each meal? Will the slow and steady eaters get any food at all if you include a number of fast-swimming greedy species? Will that harmless but large and boisterous fish you like the look of frighten the life out of smaller, shyer tankmates? These are all questions that must be answered.

Never make any assumptions on the basis of apparently successful and uneventful cohabitation in a dealer's tank; the fishes' behaviour may be affected by relative crowding, lack of decor, and by their age (often fishes offered for sale are subadult). Give them space, something to fight over, and a few months' growth, and the story may be quite different!

Making Your Selection

In making your selection, don't let your reading stop at this volume. There is a considerable amount of aquarium literature available, ranging from assorted magazines to a host of specialized books on specific groups of fishes. You do not have to buy them – simply ask your local library to obtain them for you. You can also visit public aquaria and aquatic retailers to see some of the fishes in the flesh.

Don't succumb to your understandable impatience to get up and running – this preliminary research should be regarded as all part of the fun. Patience is an essential quality to cultivate if you want to succeed, so the sooner you practise it the better! We cannot over-emphasize the importance of getting everything right first time. There is no

Anemone fishes, such as this *Amphiprion* species (clownfish) live in symbiosis with sea anemones on their native coral reefs. A suitable anemone must, therefore, be provided for the clownfish in captivity.

point in setting up your tank and then finding it won't do for the fishes you want to keep; that will mean settling for second best or starting again from scratch. Get it wrong and you risk causing suffering to your fishes, not to mention wasting your time and money; what should have been a source of immense enjoyment for many years could turn into a nightmare.

Far too many aquarists set about the task in completely the opposite fashion, setting up an aquarium and populating it with whatever their local pet shop has to offer that month. Only later do they realize what they are missing when they see a fish they really like, often totally unsuitable for their aquarium. The sensible few go home and find out about their dream fish – *before* buying it. The majority, regrettably, take it home without doing any homework, usually discovering their error the hard way – upsetting for the aquarist, but catastrophic for the fishes.

Be assured, we do not exaggerate. Every year we receive numerous letters from aquarists asking us if the fishes they have bought will live together harmoniously, or, all too often, why their chosen combination has proved disastrous. Others set up an aquarium and then ask if it is suitable for the fishes they fancy. While we have no desire to put ourselves out of a job, we would prefer it if people would find out first!

The Fishkeeping Network

Apart from books, there is another invaluable source of information available to you – the accumulated knowledge of other aquarists, both professional (dealers) and other amateurs like yourself. Fishkeeping is a friendly hobby, and you will find that most enthusiasts are more than willing to help. If it was seeing a friend's aquarium that stimulated your interest in the first place, don't be afraid to go back to him or her and pick his or her brains. He or she may know other aquarists who will be only too happy to let you see their set-ups

Killifishes are beautiful but usually shortlived; their native pools dry up in summer, and only their eggs survive until the rains come.

Above: Poecilia reticulata (the guppy) is a very popular and easy-to-maintain livebearer. Numerous varieties are available, but although they are all very easy to breed, carefully planned line-breeding is needed to produce quality stock.

Below: A well-planted freshwater aquarium is a miniature underwater garden, and an ornament to any home.

Above left: Botia macracantha (the clown loach) is often kept singly, but actually prefers the company of its own kind. It grows rather larger than many aquarists realize.

and answer your questions. Consider joining your local aquarists' club – you will be made welcome even though you don't yet have any fishes of your own. Such clubs exist in most large towns and cities, although it is not always easy to obtain a contact address. Local aquarium shops may be able to help; if not, most countries have a national federation of fishkeeping clubs which can supply details, and whose contact address can usually be found in fishkeeping magazines.

Even if you are not by nature the sociable type, there are many advantages, apart from shared knowledge, to belonging to a club. If you have fishkeeping friends then you have people you can call upon in all sorts of otherwise difficult situations – getting a large tank home and into place; looking after your fishes while you are on holiday; helping out if some vital item of equipment fails at 3 am on Sunday morning. There is the possibility of spare equipment and home-bred fishes at bargain prices, and perhaps the loan of extra reading material.

The Aquatic Dealer

It will also be to your immense advantage to find a good aquatic dealer and make a friend of him. You will need guidance when it comes to buying equipment, because the quantity and variety available nowadays is confusing even to the expert, and positively daunting to the beginner. He will be able to advise what is best suited to your particular circumstances, and what brands are most reliable. A good dealer is also a mine of information on fishes and fishkeeping. You may not buy all your fishes from him (he may not have what you want – though if you are a good customer he may get it for you), but you should reward his investment of time and patience in you, his customer, by always going to him for "dry goods". He may not be right on your doorstep, but his help will more than recompense you for any expenditure in time and travel.

So, how do you find a suitable dealer? Firstly, ask other aquarists for a recommendation. Failing that, the most important difference between a good dealer and a bad one is one of attitude. Both have a living to make, but money is the chief motivation of the bad dealer. He will rarely be prepared to spend time talking. Don't expect him to net out a particular fish from a batch of 20 – it will be too much trouble. He will grumble if you insist on a pair, even if the species is easily sexed. He will allow you to buy any combination of equipment and fishes without question.

Small tetras such as those pictured above should never be housed with *Astronotus ocellatus* (oscars), although unscrupulous dealers may sell both together as suitable for the general community tank.

The honest dealer, by contrast, will try to deter you from any folly, and perhaps even refuse to sell – he values his reputation and integrity more than the proverbial quick buck. If he can't answer your questions, he will get a book out. Ask for two fishes, and he will catch you a pair if they are sexable. He will be patient and will take time to talk, even if you are a stranger who may never darken his doors again – and he will probably recognize you when you do go back.

If in doubt, try going along with an outrageous shopping list of totally incompatible fishes (we suggest, for example, the oscar cichlid and the neon tetra), and let it be known that you have just (yesterday) set up a 60-cm (24-inch) tank and intend introducing both to it immediately. The bad dealer won't bat an eyelid and will get out his nets and polythene bags. The good one will politely, but firmly, read you the riot act.

Water Management

Water is an essential constituent of all life forms; to fishes, however, it is environmental as well as metabolic – the medium in which they live, just as we live in air. Like us, fishes pass water through their excretory and alimentary tracts; but they also "breathe" it, using their gills (and sometimes other organs) to extract essential oxygen and discharge carbon dioxide. There is also an exchange of metabolic and environmental water by osmosis.

We become uncomfortable or ill if we drink polluted water, or if the air we breathe doesn't suit our individual preferences (usually what we are used to) or the general requirements of our species – it may be too hot, cold, still, windy, dry, or humid for our liking, too low in oxygen, or polluted with smoke or toxic gases. Air, however, has a fairly uniform chemical composition throughout the world, so someone from one part of our planet can survive in any other, though he or she may find the local climate unpleasant.

Water, by contrast, is highly variable in its chemistry: it can be fresh, brackish, or saline; hard or soft; acid or alkaline; rich or poor in oxygen; pure or polluted. Unlike us, fishes are restricted in their distribution – we can go anywhere there is air, but not all bodies of water are accessible to all fishes, for reasons of geography (for example a sea fish cannot enter a land-locked lake) and environmental unsuitability. The latter is usually the end-product of the former – geological activity isolates a body of

Above: Different species of *Tetraodon* (puffers) can be found in fresh, brackish, and marine waters.
Right: Correct water chemistry and A1 water quality are absolutely essential when dealing with sensitive coral fishes and invertebrates.

Gouramis such as *Trichogaster trichopterus* (three spot gourami) come from muddy, oxygen-depleted waters, and have an accessory respiratory organ (the labyrinth) which enables them to breathe atmospheric air. They will not, however, be inconvenienced by the water clarity and ample oxygen levels required by other community fishes.

water and its fauna; subsequently there is gradual modification of water parameters (chemistry, temperature, quality) paralleled by adaptation of the fishes to the changing conditions. Their systems, thus specialized, are then often unable to cope with any subsequent change. They may suffer discomfort or poor health, or even die, if the water in which they find themselves – which they "drink" and "breathe" and which interacts with their body fluids – does not meet their specific requirements – especially if the change is abrupt.

We must therefore never assume that water is a uniform element, or that any fish will live happily in what comes out of the tap. The aquarist must be a "water technician", providing the correct environment in terms of chemistry, temperature, oxygen content, movement, and freedom from pollution ("water quality"). There are instruments and test kits for monitoring aquarium water, and a huge variety of equipment for adjusting its chemistry, quality, and other factors, so there is no excuse for hit-and-miss water management.

Water Chemistry

This is the term used by aquarists to describe the combined salinity, hardness, and acidity/alkalinity (pH) of water. For a fish to survive its metabolism must be in tune with these aspects of its environment, and successful adaptation to significant alterations normally requires changes to be gradual, allowing time for metabolic adjustment. Sudden change can be fatal if a fish's organs cannot cope with the altered environment ("chemical shock"). While some fishes can be adapted to "unnatural" water chemistry, this may prove detrimental in the long term; and the difference between certain environments, for example salt and fresh water, are too great to overcome.

There are two sensible ways of approaching this question of water chemistry: you can either keep fishes suited to the water you can provide from the tap, or modify your local water to meet the needs of more demanding species. Modification of water chemistry can be expensive and time-consuming, with the possibility of error, so we suggest that beginners take the former course. We do not recommend the third option of attempting to modify the fishes!

Your dealer should be able to tell you which species are "hardy", and which will not live long in your tap water. Even so, check whether the hardy types are actually found in water similar to yours in the wild – if not you may still need to modify it for breeding. Some species occur naturally in several different bodies of water sometimes offering quite diverse environments. Without specific data on origin the best approach is to create average conditions for the species, modifying these slowly if the fish appears unhappy.

Chemicals which can be used to alter water chemistry. Marine salt (*bottom left*) for increasing salinity; Sodium bicarbonate (*top left*) for increasing pH; proprietary pH adjusters come in tablet (*top right*) or powder (*bottom right*) form.

In nature *Dimidiochromis compressiceps* (the Malawian eyebiter) feeds on the fry of other species and is reputed to eat the eyes of adults. In captivity it is rather timid, and does not behave "antisocially" if well fed. It should, however, be kept only with other Malawi cichlids, and like them requires moderately hard, alkaline, well-oxygenated, water.

Sudden increases in hardness or dramatic alterations in pH are the changes most likely to have dire effects; even natural water chemistry may prove harmful if the fishes' systems have adjusted to different conditions. Local shops usually use tap water (except for marines and some delicate freshwater species – do check in each case), so it may be best to do likewise initially and gradually adjust water chemistry after introducing the fishes. Later on you may wish to buy additional fishes, possibly accustomed to different conditions to those now prevailing in your aquarium. In such cases set up a temporary tank with conditions suited to the new arrivals, then adjust water chemistry gradually to match your main aquarium.

You may be told that chemical shock can be minimized by mixing small amounts of aquarium water with that in the bag prior to releasing fishes. That is rubbish – the necessary metabolic adjustment takes days or weeks, not minutes.

Let us now look at the various aspects of water chemistry in more detail:

Overpage: *Microgeophagus ramirezi* (the ram or butterfly cichlid) requires soft, acid water to thrive. The other fishes seen here come from the same type of biotope, but are "hardier".

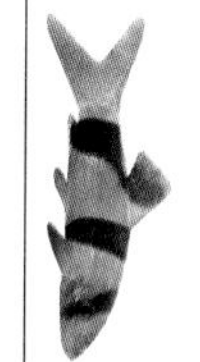

Salinity

This is the measure of common salt (sodium chloride, NaCl) content, and is normally applied only to salt and brackish water (fresh water, by definition, does not contain measurable quantities of NaCl). It is measured using a hydrometer. Nowadays, because of coastal pollution, water for the marine or brackish aquarium is normally "created" (rather than collected), using tap water and special "marine salts" containing not only sodium chloride but also desirable trace elements. Instructions are normally provided, but the salinity of the mix should always be checked. (It is important to remember never to use "domestic" salt, which may contain additives toxic to fishes.)

Most killifishes (this is *Nothobranchius furzeri*) require soft, acid water...

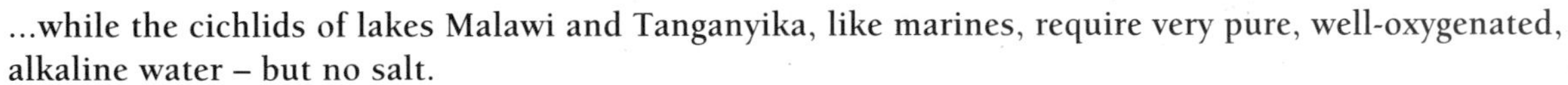

...while the cichlids of lakes Malawi and Tanganyika, like marines, require very pure, well-oxygenated, alkaline water – but no salt.

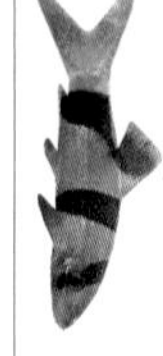

Hardness

Hardness is the measure of dissolved mineral salts (mainly chlorides, bicarbonates, carbonates, and sulphates of calcium, sodium, magnesium, and potassium); the harder the water the more salts it contains. It is generally expressed in terms of calcium carbonate ($CaCO_3$) content, measured in degrees (dH) or parts per million (ppm) using a special test kit. Care is needed with regard to "degrees of hardness", the definition of which varies from country to country and test kit to test kit, depending on origin.

Water becomes hard by dissolving soluble salts from the rocks or soil over or through which it flows. Some rocks, for example slate, granite, and gneiss, contain little or no soluble material and have a negligible effect, while others, notably limestones, are quite the opposite. Rocks and other "hard" decor in the aquarium may affect water chemistry: corals and shells are largely calcium carbonate, and gravel often contains fragments of limestone or shell. Hardness-free decor is a prerequisite of the soft-water aquarium.

It is easy to harden soft water with lime-rich decor or the special salt mixes (*not* marine salt) available for simulating conditions in east African lakes, and, as luck would have it, fishes from hard water seem not to suffer any ill-effects from softer-than-natural conditions (but see pH, below). Unfortunately the reverse does not apply: reducing hardness is troublesome, and soft-water fishes often fail to thrive in hard conditions.

Some waters, such as this high moorland stream, are acidified by the peat bogs across which they flow.

Using a Test Kit

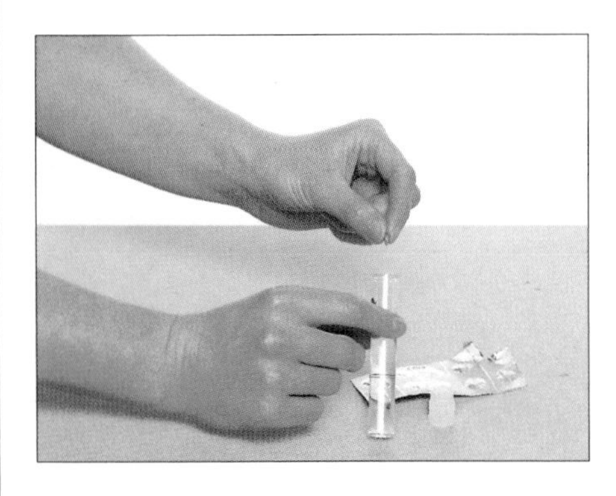

1 Add the reagent – which can be a tablet, as here, or a liquid from a bottle – to a measured sample of water in the vial supplied.

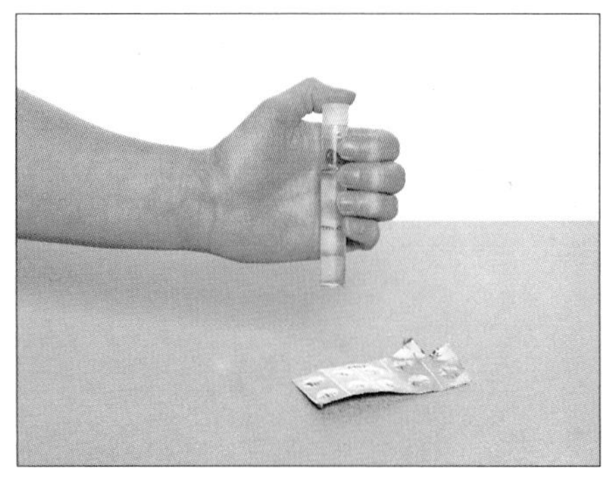

2 Replace the cap on the vial and vigorously shake the reagent/water for a few seconds to mix properly.

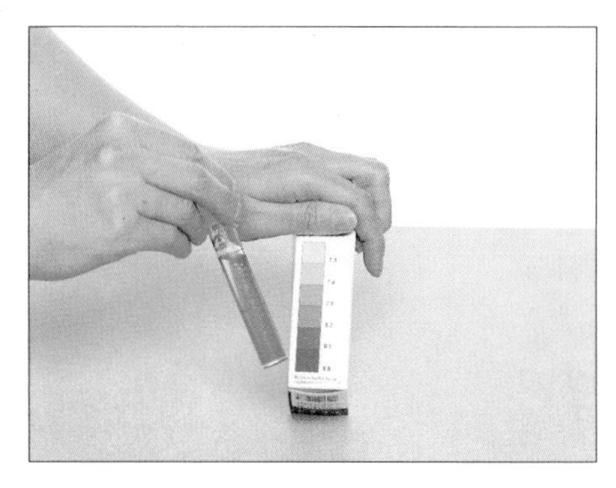

3 Once the time required for the necessary reaction has elapsed, compare the colour of the sample with the colour on the chart provided.

Softening Water

There are various methods of softening water:

1 By boiling, which removes some, but not all, of the dissolved salts.

2 By dilution with rain water. This is the cheapest method, the only outlay being suitable containers, made of non-toxic material, for collecting and storing water. Roofs, gutters, and downpipes must be as clean as possible, and avoid cemented roofs as cement is powdered limestone. Water collected close to, or downwind of, industrial areas may be polluted. Collect only during prolonged downpours, and wait a few minutes while dust and any other rubbish is washed away. It is advisable to strain the water through filter floss straight away to remove any stray detritus. Rain water may carry the risk of pollution, but so may tap water (see below).

3 By dilution with artificially softened water. This may be: a) distilled; b) softened using an ion-exchange resin (use only resins sold for aquarium use). This may affect pH, and, as it exchanges calcium ions for (usually) sodium ions, the result may be soft but still mineral-rich (and unsuitable for fishes from mineral-poor waters); c) processed by a reverse osmosis unit, available from aquatic retailers (but expensive). This removes all minerals but is wasteful – some 45.5 litres (10 gallons) of tap water are needed to produce 4.5 litres (1 gallon) of mineral-free water.

The collected or treated water can be used "neat" to create very soft conditions. Distilled and reverse-osmosis water should *never* be used "neat"; not, as often stated, because they contain no minerals, but because both processes remove free oxygen so there is nothing to "breathe". Aerate thoroughly before use to rectify this problem.

You may come across the following additional terms: "Temporary hardness" is that which can be removed by boiling, while "permanent hardness" is that which cannot. "Carbonate hardness" (KH) is that contributed by (bi)carbonates, but not other salts such as sulphates and chlorides. "General hardness" (GH) includes all dissolved salts, and is sometimes referred to as "total hardness" or "total dissolved salts" (TDS). Scientists often measure mineral content in terms not of hardness but of electrical conductivity, the units employed being micro-siemens (μS).

***Sphaerichthys osphronemoides* (the chocolate gourami) requires specific water conditions, unlike most other popular anabantids.**

pH

The pH scale is used to indicate the acidity or alkalinity of a substance; it runs from 0 to 14, 0 being the extreme of acidity, 14 that of alkalinity, and 7 neutral. Most fishes come from waters with a pH between 5.5 and 9.0, although there are outliers at either end of the scale. It is vital to remember that the scale is logarithmic – each step up or down from neutral is 10 times the previous one: pH 4 is 10 times more acid than pH 5, and 100 times more acid than pH 6. Apparently small variations can thus have dramatic effects on fishes. Luckily the scale is the universally accepted method of measuring acidity/alkalinity, so there is no problem with different units as with hardness. Special test kits are available and affluent aquarists may wish to buy electronic pH meters.

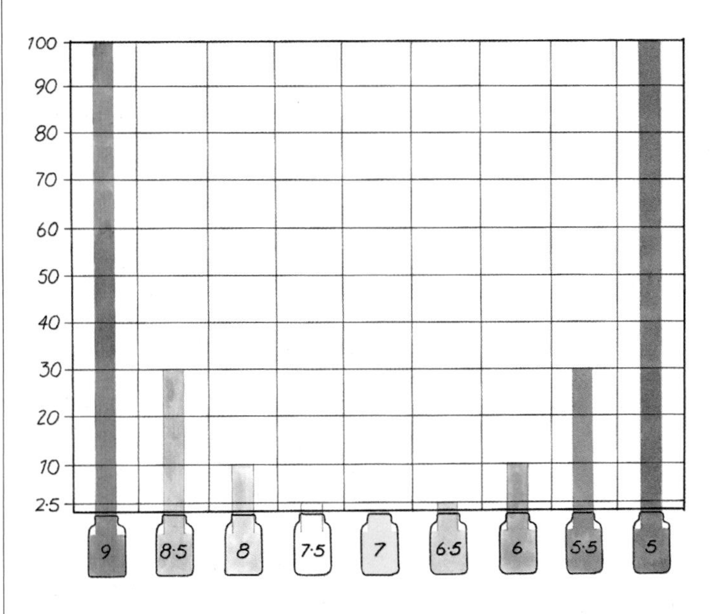

pH Scale chart

The pH of water is affected by substances dissolved in it. The salts which harden water usually also render it alkaline; soft water, by contrast, is often slightly acid, because rain reacts with atmospheric carbon dioxide to form dilute carbonic acid. Decaying organic material, such as is found in peat bogs and forests, acidifies water flowing through such areas.

There is little point in trying to acidify aquarium water which is being constantly buffered back to neutral or alkaline by dissolved salts derived from tap water or the decor. First minimize hardness, otherwise you are wasting your time. Soft water is easily acidified using peat filtration (see below). Loose peat will "migrate" and is best placed in a nylon bag (a stocking will do), and the whole rinsed to remove tiny particles. Peat is fairly quickly "exhausted" and needs renewing at intervals established by monitoring pH.

Water can be made alkaline by using calciferous decor or by filtering over coral, crushed shell, or limestone chips. Such material should always be included in systems for fishes which cannot tolerate acid conditions, to act as a buffer against the acidifying effects of metabolic byproducts.

Using Peat as a Filter Medium

1 Peat needs to be contained in a fine-meshed bag in order to prevent it escaping from the filter. A section of nylon stocking is ideal for the purpose.

2 Push the peat into the nylon stocking, packing down tightly. Once the bag is filled tie a knot in the open end.

3 Rinse under the tap or in a bucket of water to remove any particles. The bag of peat can then be used in a box filter, or in most types of canister filter.

Above: **Always dissolve bicarbonate of soda in a little water before use. The solution can be mixed with the new water for the aquarium and an accurate test result achieved. Adding the "bicarb" dry risks incorrect test results if some remains undissolved at the time of the test.**

These methods are gradual in effect; to avoid "pH shock" when you change part of the aquarium water you may need to adjust the pH of the "new" water rapidly before use (though in practice partial water changes with neutral water rarely have any ill-effect). If you use a proprietary "pH adjuster" follow the instructions to the letter – failure to do so may prove fatal for the fishes. We prefer to prepare new water in advance (leaving it to stand over peat or calciferous material), or to use bicarbonate of soda ($NaHCO_3$) to raise pH, or peat extract (made by boiling peat) to lower it. Dosage must be established initially by adding small amounts to the new water and measuring the pH. Always treat the water *before* adding it to the aquarium.

Water chemistry is in fact far more complex than we have intimated, because mineral composition (the salts contributing to the hardness) varies considerably from area to area. There is, however, rarely any need to simulate the exact formulation, as fishes are able to extract the amount of each vital element they actually require.

In nature the volume of water relative to fish populations, together with the action of plants in removing wastes, ensures adequate water quality.

Water Quality

Water quality is equally as important as chemistry. Most of the complexities of the latter can be avoided by keeping fishes suited to local water, but providing and maintaining good water quality is a continuing process. This falls into two parts: ensuring no harmful chemicals enter the aquarium from outside; and dealing with waste products produced by its occupants. Many fishes come from virtually unpolluted water and are highly sensitive to any contaminants. Some are more tolerant, but it is nevertheless unwise to provide less than optimal water quality in captivity – the sheer volume of natural waters acts as a safety net, whereas any problem can rapidly escalate in the restricted capacity of the aquarium.

All equipment and decor must be non-toxic – where possible use items intended specifically for aquarium use. "Non-aquatic" plastics should ideally be "food quality"; avoid coloured types, especially those with a nasty taste. Metals may corrode (especially in salt water), producing toxic salts, so use only those metal items designed for aquarium use (for example aluminium hoods) and always check suitability for marine aquaria. Rocks should not (unintentionally) affect the water, but beware of coloured crystals which may be poisonous. Garden items (such as flowerpots and stones) may be contaminated with pesticides or fertilizers. Wood (for example hoods) may leach tannins, or worse, preservatives, unless coated with polyurethane varnish. Insecticide aerosols, spray polishes, paint fumes, and other domestic chemicals can poison fishes. A definitive list is impossible, so always be on your guard.

As if this were not enough, the water from your tap may contain invisible nasty surprises. Water that has stood in metal pipes may be tainted with

Although *Carassius auratus* (the goldfish) is a cold water fish, some fancy varieties are prone to fin-rot if exposed to very low temperatures.

metallic oxide. This contamination is normally slight but can accumulate in the aquarium, so run the tap for a while before using any water. Never use water from a copper hot-water cylinder.

Water companies are required to provide water "of potable quality". This does not always equate with aquarium quality, as chemical treatments and pollution levels deemed harmless to humans can be lethal to fishes. The commonest additive is chlorine gas, highly toxic to fishes but easily dealt with: if water is left to stand for 24 hours the gas will disperse into the air. The process can be speeded up by aeration, and if chlorine content is low (the gas can't be smelt), it is often sufficient to run the tap hard into a bucket. Some water companies now use an alternative, far more toxic, purification agent, chloramine, which does not disperse naturally. Water conditioners are available (from your local dealer) to neutralize this chemical, as well as chlorine. Ask your water company if they use chloramine or intend to do so, and ask to be warned whenever they intend to flush the mains to eliminate aquatic invertebrates, as the DDT used is toxic to fishes. Be friendly and polite – their only obligation is to provide drinkable water. Help with your fishes is voluntary.

Tap water may contain nitrates and phosphates (the result of agricultural fertilizers leaching into rivers and aquifers, or of incomplete "purification" during recycling), especially when water levels are low and pollutant concentrations correspondingly high; fortunate the aquarist whose tap water originates from a moorland reservoir or other uncontaminated source. Nitrate test kits are available from dealers. Nitrates should be removed from water intended for the aquarium reverse osmosis, or a special filter connected to the tap.

The Nitrogen Cycle

However good your initial water quality, it will deteriorate when fishes are introduced. Fishes excrete wastes, plants lose leaves, and inevitably there will be particles of food uneaten. In both nature and the aquarium such detritus is broken down by bacteria during a series of processes termed the nitrogen cycle. The first stage in this cycle is highly toxic ammonia (and its compounds), excreted by fishes and produced by the decomposition of organic matter; this is rapidly converted to nitrites (still dangerously toxic), which are in turn processed into nitrates. These are relatively harmless, though sudden or long-term exposure to high concentrations can be harmful.

Although the nitrogen cycle will operate in any mature aquarium, fish population density is generally higher than in a comparable volume of water in nature, so the system is unbalanced; a tank may look clean but have high levels of ammonia or nitrite. Action is necessary to redress the balance and avoid such problems. The process normally used is filtration, during which the aquarium water is passed through one or more materials (filter media) to remove wastes. There are three main types of filtration – mechanical, chemical, and biological – and aquarium systems are usually a combination of at least two of these.

Nitrogen Cycle in the Aquarium

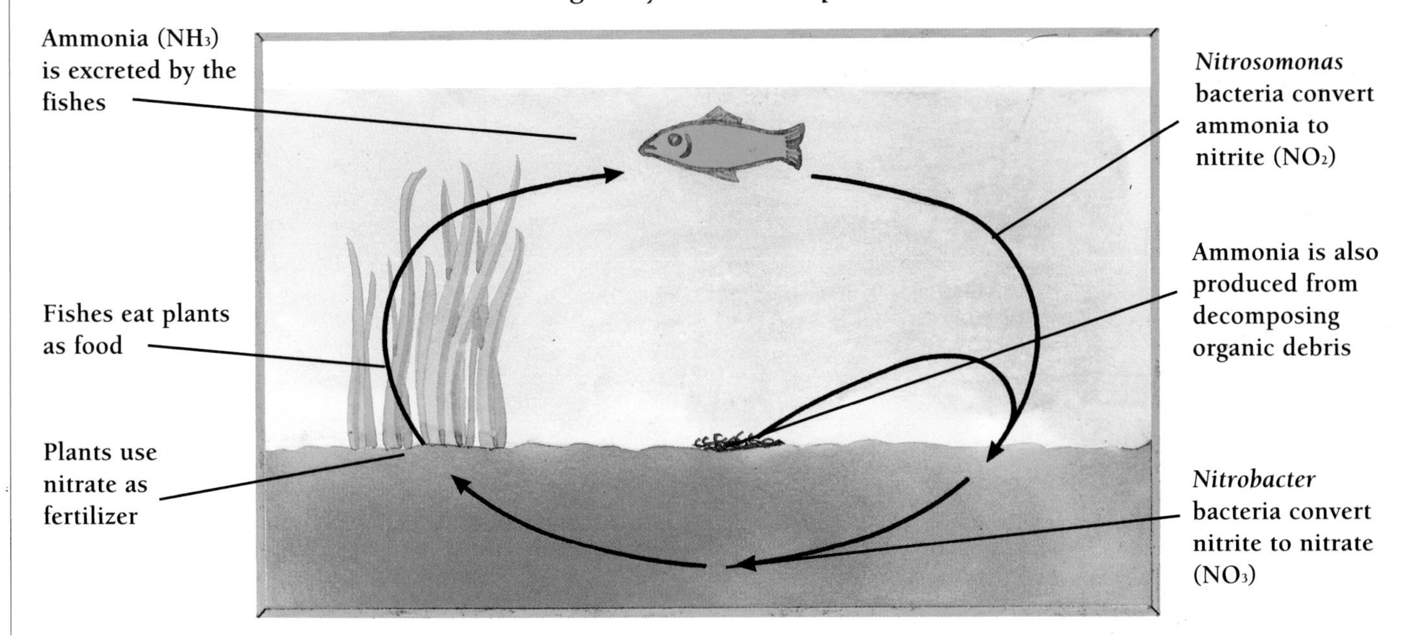

Types of Filtration

Mechanical Filtration: During mechanical filtration solids are trapped by the filter; they are, however, still part of the aquarium system until the medium is replaced or cleaned, just as dust swept under the carpet is still in the house! The commonest media used are filter floss, plastic foam, and gravel/sand.

Chemical Filtration: This process uses media which alter the chemical composition of the water, for example the alteration of pH using peat or lime-rich material, reduction of hardness by ion-exchange resins, and removal of metabolic products by activated carbon or zeolite (which remove carbon dioxide and ammonia respectively). Chemical media also trap solids mechanically.

Biological Filtration: Biological filtration involves enhancing natural populations of the bacteria which operate the nitrogen cycle by providing the conditions they require – surfaces to colonize, supplies of wastes to process, and, for those which convert nitrites to nitrates, a constant supply of oxygen. The filter medium offers living space, and the flow of water through the filter ensures a constant supply of wastes and oxygen. Biological filtration takes place in any mechanical or chemical filter which has been left undisturbed long enough to develop a bacterial population, and the media used in biological filters also have a mechanical (and sometimes chemical) effect. As well as those already mentioned there are plastic, ceramic, and glass media, all of which maximize the surface area available for colonization. Efficient biological filtration is the key to maintaining water quality on a day-to-day basis.

The nitrogen cycle must be considered when planning and maintaining a filtration system, as whether you want biological filtration or not you are going to get it! It takes about two weeks for the nitrogen cycle to become properly functional in a new system (aquarium and filter(s)); fishes cannot be introduced until after this maturation period because of ammonia/nitrate toxicity. If the established nitrogen cycle is subsequently interrupted there will again be a risk of toxicity. This commonly happens when "dirty" filters are cleaned because they are considered to be unhygienic and life-threatening; in fact most of the "dirt" in a mature filter is the inert (and harmless) residue left by bacterial processing. Removing it does nothing to improve hygiene, but the accompanying elimination of the established bacterial population can wreak havoc. It is, however, sometimes necessary to clean filters if clogging by inert matter is impeding flow, or if chemical media are exhausted. Only part (50 per cent maximum) of the filter contents should be cleaned or replaced; this will leave an adequate residual bacterial population, but feeding should nevertheless be reduced for a few days to lighten the load on the biological system while it regenerates to full strength.

FILTER MEDIA

ammonia remover

gravel

peat

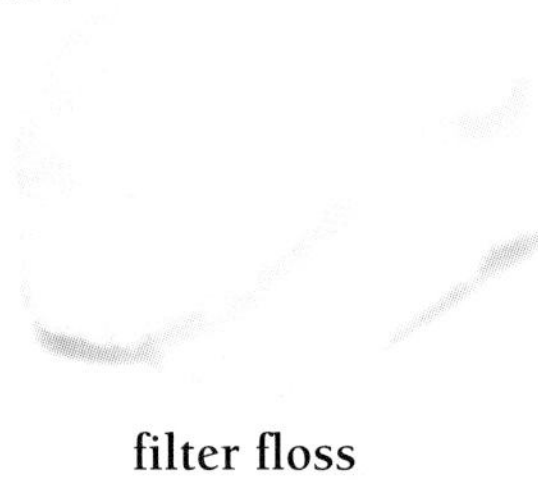

filter floss

activated carbon

limestone chips

coral sand

foam

ceramic tubes

All filter media act mechanically, straining solids from the water. If the filter is allowed to mature all media will likewise be colonized by beneficial bacteria. Some, for example the hexagonal ceramic tubes shown here, are specifically designed to optimize bacterial activity. Some chemical media (for example carbon and ammonia remover (zeolite)), remove certain toxins, while others (for example peat, limestone chips, coral sand), are used to adjust hardness and/or pH.

Types of Filter

Canister Filters: These are self-contained units with a container (the filter chamber) for media and an electric pump to circulate water. They may be external, with inlet and outlet pipes from and to the aquarium, or internal, with slits to allow water into the filter and an outlet from the pump. They combine mechanical and biological filtration, with chemical optional. Special external filters using diatomaceous earth optimize water clarity by mechanically removing particles but are expensive to run and need frequent maintenance as they clog rapidly.

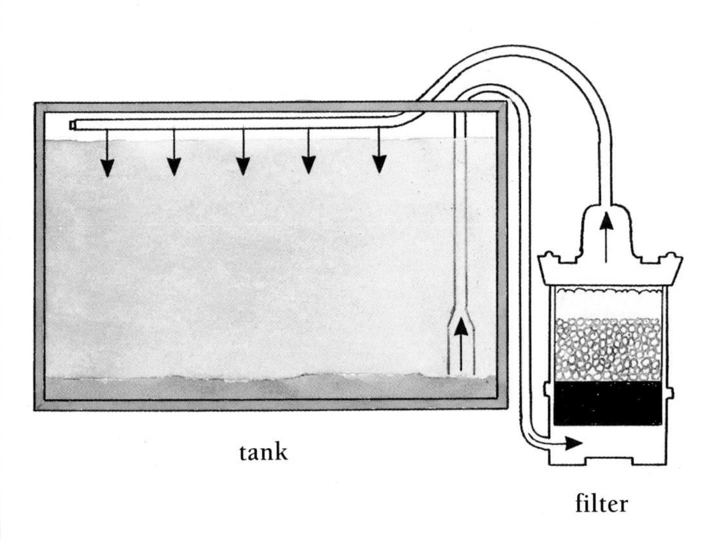

Canister filter

Canister filters are mechanical and biological, sometimes chemical, in operation. Water is siphoned out of the aquarium into the filter canister, then pumped up through the filter media and back to the aquarium, in this case via a spray bar.

Undergravel (UG) Filters: UG filters consist of a plastic plate positioned between the aquarium bottom and the substrate, with one or more uplift pipes. Water is drawn down through the substrate and returned via the uplift(s). UG filters can be powered by: a) the airlift principle (rising bubbles of air draw water with them), an airline being inserted in the uplift tube; b) powerheads, electric pumps which fit on to the uplift tubes; or c) an external canister filter with its inlet tube inserted in the uplift. The substrate, which should be 5-7.5 cm (2-3 inches) deep for maximum effectiveness, acts as the filter medium, and its action is both mechanical and biological, sometimes chemical. The advantages of undergravel filtration are that the "inlet" is the entire aquarium bottom so wastes cannot escape processing, and the large amount of filter medium available for bacterial colonization. The main disadvantage is that when the system eventually becomes clogged cleaning involves a major upheaval.

A reverse-flow UG system minimizes this problem by using an external canister filter as a mechanical pre-filter, the outlet being attached to the UG uplift so that water is pumped up through the substrate. This unfortunately also negates the advantage of UG – the system inlet is now that of the pre-filter, which is also probably the main site of bacterial activity! Reverse-flow systems create no surface turbulence and this may result in oxygen depletion unless the aquarium is aerated independently of the filtration system.

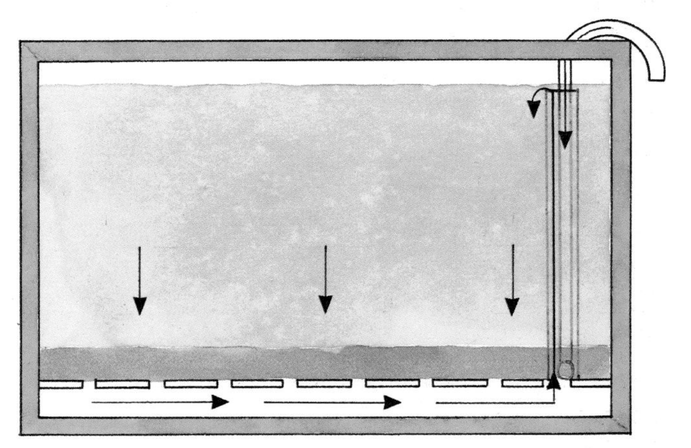

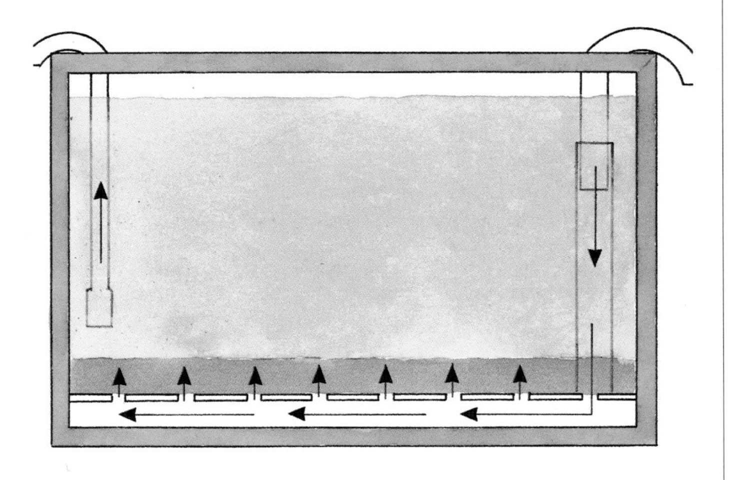

Undergravel Flows

In conventional flow UG (*top*) water is drawn <u>down</u> through the filter bed (substrate) and <u>up</u> the uplift pipe (by airlift or powerhead). In reverse flow (*bottom*) a canister filter pumps water <u>down</u> the uplift and <u>up</u> through the substrate.

Trickle Filters: These consist of one or more trays with perforated bottoms, part-filled with filter media, stacked above the aquarium, and used in conjunction with an external canister filter, whose return is sprayed on to the (top) tray and trickles back into the tank via the perforations. The water is thus exposed to air, optimizing its oxygen uptake and hence bacterial activity. A further advantage is that its capacity (the volume of media) can be increased by means of additional trays without the need to increase turnover (water flow rate). Trickle filters may alternatively be situated beneath the aquarium, with the water being siphoned into the filter and pumped back.

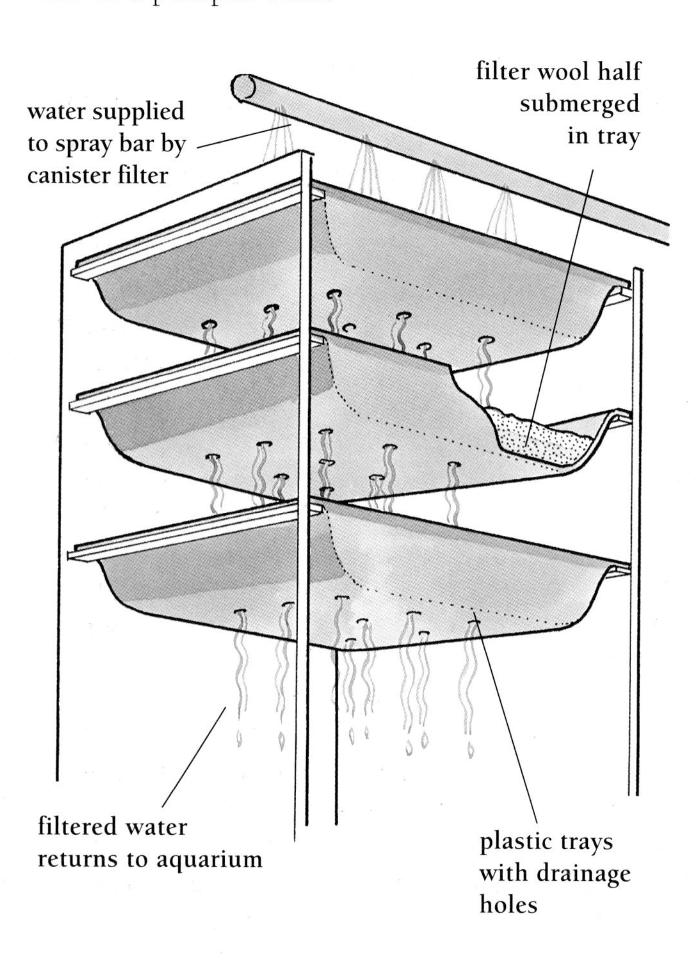

Trickle Filter

Trickle filters are usually sited on top of the aquarium and fed by the return from a canister filter (spray bar). Water and filter media are exposed to atmospheric oxygen, making for excellent biological efficiency.

Box Filters: Box filters may be internal or external and are driven by the airlift principle. They have, however, largely been superseded by more complex systems, but the internal type is still useful for small tanks, tanks with minimal loading, and supplementary chemical filtration.

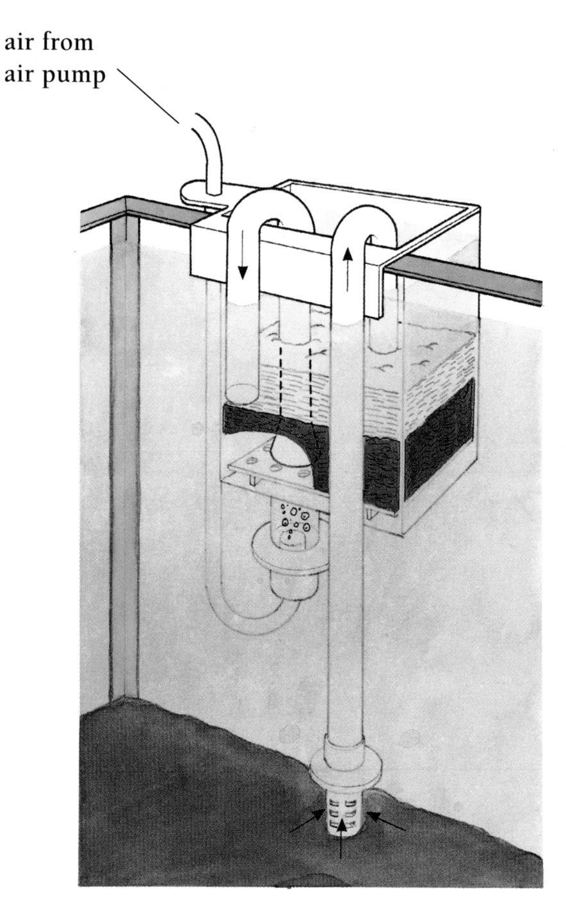

External Box Filter

Water is siphoned out of the aquarium, descends through the filter media, and is returned via an airlift.

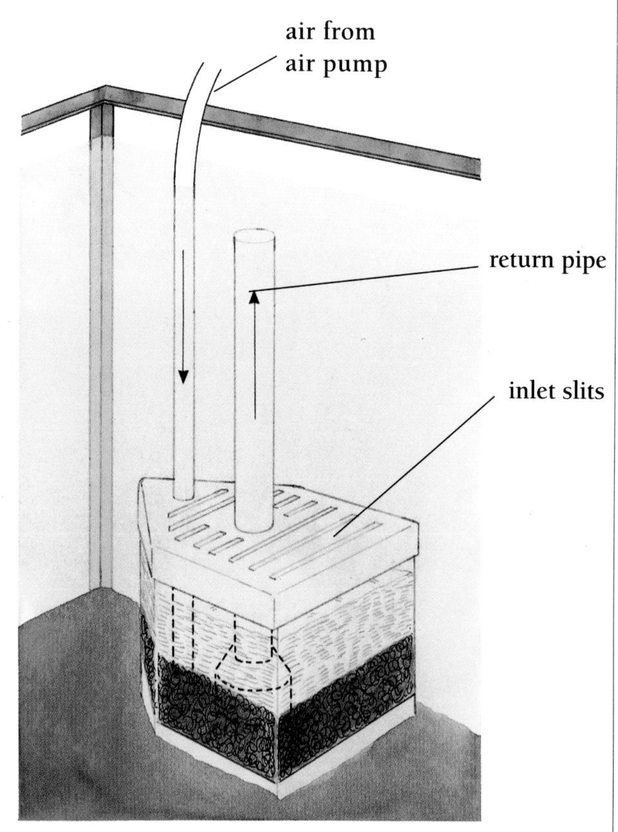

Internal Box Filter

The airlift principle is used to draw water down through the filter and up the return pipe.

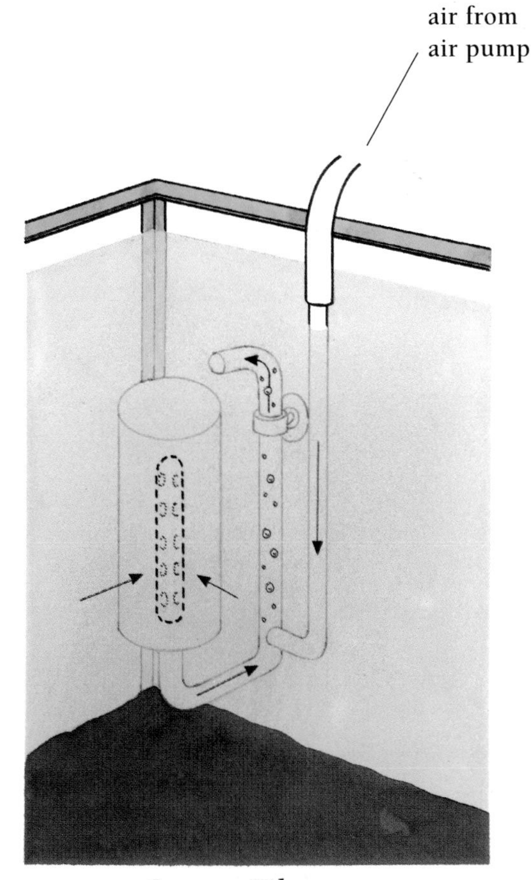

Sponge Filter

Sponge filters are ideal for small aquaria.

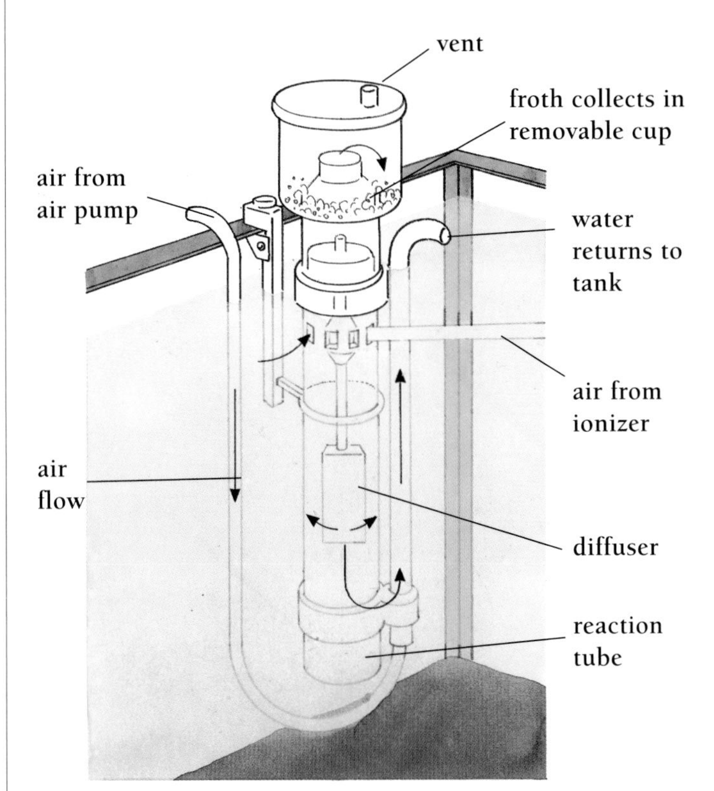

Protein Skimmer

Protein skimmers work only in salt water and are essential for marine aquaria.

Sponge Filters: A sponge filter consists of a perforated plastic tube fitted with a cylindrical sponge. Air is passed through the tube, drawing water through the sponge. These filters act mechanically and biologically; they are best suited to aquaria with low filtration needs.

Protein Skimmers: Protein skimmers, essential in the marine aquarium, utilize a process known as "air stripping". Proteins and other organics adhere to air bubbles, forming a foam which rises to the top of the unit to be collected in a removable container which is emptied at least once a day. They do not work in fresh water.

Optimizing Water Quality

The amount and type of filtration required depends on the nature of the individual aquarium. Biological efficiency is a function of bacterial population size, in turn dependent on available colonizable area (filter capacity) and oxygen supply – not, as many aquarists assume, purely on turnover rate. In choosing a filtration system take into consideration tank size, probable metabolic loading (number, sizes, and feeding habits of the fishes relative to water volume), and water movement requirements (of the fishes), in order to decide what filter type, capacity, and turnover rate suit your specific circumstances. Expert advice (for example from your dealer) can be invaluable. Filter efficiency can be monitored using the kits available for measuring ammonia, nitrites, and nitrates.

Although biological filtration will deal with ammonia and nitrites, it will not eliminate nitrates, and without additional action a gradual build-up of these is inevitable, even if some are utilized by plants. Although nitrates are relatively harmless, long-term exposure to high concentrations may shorten lifespan and reduce resistance to disease. Sudden exposure to high nitrate levels is often fatal for example if new fishes, unaccustomed to high levels, are introduced. Far too often the retailer is blamed for selling poor-quality fishes!

The most effective way of reducing nitrates (you cannot eliminate them altogether in a functioning system) is to replace part of the aquarium water regularly; how much and how often depends on the individual tank, but 20 per cent weekly is a good starting point. Monitoring with a test kit will indicate whether the routine needs to be modified. It is inadvisable to change more than a third of the water at a time, and replacement water should be

Filling an Internal Box Filter

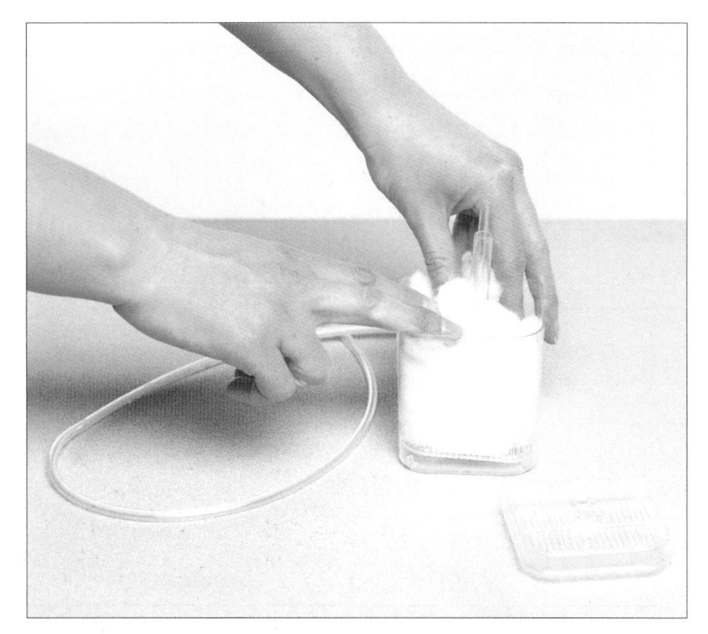

1 Internal box filters are often used as additional chemical filters, filled with peat, zeolite, carbon, or another chemical medium. Filled with filter floss, however, they are perfectly suited to small aquaria. Fit the uplift section into the box and pack the medium round it.

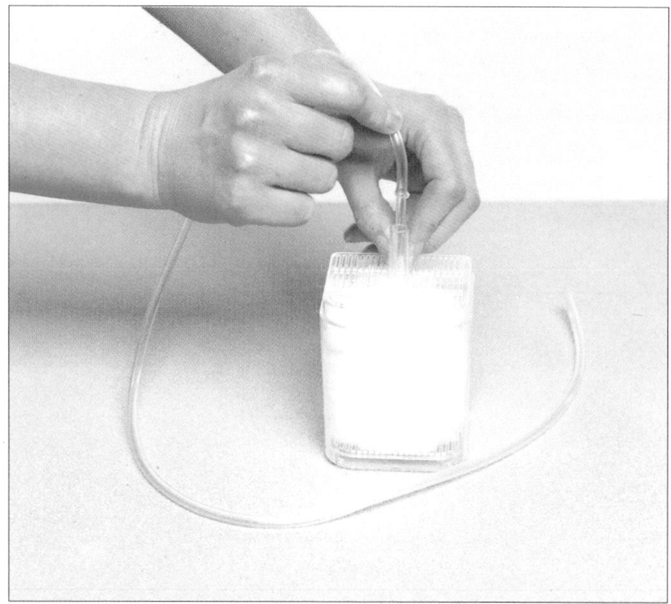

2 The filter wool should be firmly packed down into the filter. Then fit the top and attach the airline to the air supply tube. The filter is now ready to be installed in the aquarium.

detoxified (if necessary) and be of the correct chemistry and temperature. Although chemical media are available for removing nitrates, fresh water is preferable because it has the added benefit of stimulating fishes and replenishing minerals exhausted by them. Just topping up to replace water lost by evaporation does not constitute a partial water change, because any chemicals (whether organic – for example nitrates – or inorganic) are left behind during evaporation and so remain in the water.

Other Aspects of Water Management

Fishes have evolved to function at particular temperature ranges just as they have adapted to local water chemistries. In nature, variation within a species' acceptable range is normally gradual; sudden changes (as inflicted by careless aquarists) may be harmful, with a rapid drop in temperature more serious than a rise. There are species-dependent upper and lower limits above and below which metabolic failure (and death) are probable, but most species will continue to function (at least for a while) at temperatures slightly outside their optimal range. They may be sluggish if the temperature is abnormally low (never skimp on heating), and suffer respiratory distress if it is higher than normal: increased temperature results in increased metabolic rate and hence oxygen requirement, but there is a concomitant decrease in the oxygen content of the water – so the gills need to work harder on both counts. Oxygen requirements themselves vary from species to species, yet again as a function of the natural habitat. The more turbulent the water the more rapidly it can absorb oxygen from the atmosphere and the greater its oxygen content is likely to be. The reasons for this are two-fold: first, oxygen is absorbed only at the interface between air and water (its surface), which increases in area when in motion; second, water movement speeds up circulation of the oxygen, which, in completely still water, would spread from the surface only very slowly, by diffusion.

Large bodies of water (seas, large lakes) are subject to massive water movements (tides and storms) which result in high oxygen concentrations; not surprisingly the resident fishes have adapted to these levels, and, if deprived of them,

1 Remove the top of the filter and any internal top grid (bottom right of picture) designed to keep the media in the filter canister. Instal the desired media – here a peat-filled stocking, gravel, and a topping of filter floss.

2 If using a filter with internal media containers, each can be filled with a different medium. Fit the internal top grid (if any) on top of the media.

3 Fit the rubber sealing ring to the lid, position the latter, and do up the retaining clips.

4 Attach the inlet and outlet pipes; it is easier to fill a new filter before fitting these pipes, but when the filter is subsequently cleaned they are normally left attached.

Left: Symphysodon aequifasciata (the discus) comes from still waters and does not appreciate strong currents.

Opposite above: Very large lakes are highly oxygenated through surface movement, and even have surf zones where waves break on rocky shores, as here in Lake Malawi.

Opposite below: Labeotropheus fuelleborni is a characteristic cichlid of the Lake Malawi surf zone.

may die by gradual suffocation. Some species from fast-flowing rivers may be similarly affected. At the other end of the scale there are bodies of water which contain very little oxygen, yet fishes nevertheless survive there, often because they have evolved the ability to supplement their air supply directly from the atmosphere.

It is vital to ensure suitable oxygen levels in the aquarium, using artificial aeration if necessary. The return from the filter may supply the necessary turbulence, or an airpump and aeration device (an airstone or other diffuser) can be used. Most of the uptake of oxygen results not from the rising stream of bubbles but from the turbulence created as these break the surface. Filtration and aeration also serve to circulate oxygen around the aquarium. Do, however, beware of creating unnecessary turbulence in tanks housing fishes from still waters (generally with low oxygen content) as their bodies and finnage are usually adapted to conditions in their natural habitat, and they may find it hard work to swim in a miniature jacuzzi; the resulting long-term stress may prove harmful.

To conclude this chapter, a few additional do's and don'ts. Always follow manufacturers' instructions when using chemicals, test kits, and equipment. Never guess quantities when adding chemicals - measure accurately and test the result every time. Don't however, take test results as gospel if they don't make sense (for example a zero nitrate reading) – test kits often have a shelf life, and occasionally defective batches occur. If a test result differs dramatically from what appears reasonable, test again, with another kit if necessary. Finally, do always remember the immense importance of providing water which is correct in every respect, and if in doubt, always imitate nature.

Hardness Table

1 English or Clark degree of hardness	= 14.3 ppm
1 French " " "	= 10.0 ppm
1 American " " "	= 17.1 ppm
1 German " " "	= 17.9 ppm

(Note: English, French, and American degrees of hardness are a measure of calcium carbonate ($CaCO_3$), while the German is of calcium oxide (CaO).)

Foods and Feeding

As a beginner you may be tempted to buy only proprietary dried foods, of which there are types to suit almost every variety of fish. Huge amounts of time and money have been expended in ensuring that they provide all necessary dietary elements, and, of course, are palatable. They are incredibly convenient for the aquarist *but* . . . how would you like to live your entire life on convenience foods, or even chocolate bars? You need only feed flake and live foods simultaneously to see how much fishes appreciate the "wriggle factor"

First, of course, you must consider the requirements of individual species. In their natural habitats fishes consume a variety of items – other fishes, aquatic and terrestrial invertebrates, vegetation, and so on. Some are opportunistic feeders, eating anything remotely suitable that comes along, and have a generalized digestive system to match.

Above: Gyrinocheilus aymonieri (the sucking loach or Chinese algae eater), as the name suggests, feeds largely on algae growing on rocks and branches.

Right: Not all fishes feed from the surface in nature. Although most, like these barbs, will nevertheless learn to take floating dried foods in captivity, not all are physically capable of surface feeding. Such special requirements must always be considered.

Others are highly specialized, consuming only specific items (obligatory feeding), and have evolved intestinal tracts suited to digesting only the correct diet. Thus a piscivore (fish-eater) has a short digestive tract as its high-protein food is quickly and easily digested. A herbivore, by contrast, needs a much longer intestine to handle the large quantities of relatively indigestible food it needs to consume. Feeding either of these the other's food is akin to asking a cat to eat grass or a horse meat! In practice, a piscivore will refuse vegetable material, but some species which are normally herbivorous may gorge themselves on meaty foods, sometimes suffering short-term digestive troubles and long-term problems of obesity and fatty degeneration of the tissues, these in turn resulting in sterility and shortened lifespan.

Don't forget that fishes usually follow their natural instincts where food is concerned, perhaps eating items you hadn't intended as food – usually plants and smaller fishes, though ornamental snails and even bogwood may be attacked. Bottom-sifters can totally disrupt a decorated aquarium. Never

Top: Toxotes jaculator (the archer fish) is a highly specialized predator which feeds on insects that it "shoots" down from above the surface with a jet of water.

Bottom: Some fishes, like this *Corydoras adolphoi* catfish, are bottom-sifters. They require a fine, siftable substrate and small particles of sinking food.

Top: Although live *Tubifex* worms are enjoyed by many fishes, their use carries a high risk of introducing disease; frozen or freeze-dried *Tubifex* are preferable.

Bottom: Paratheraps synspilum is a large herbivore which requires vegetable material in its diet, and may supplement this with aquarium plants if not fed properly.

blame the fishes for behaving as Nature intended – it is your fault for not doing your homework.

Feeding strategies – where, when, and how fishes feed – are also important. Some feed at the surface, some in mid-water, others on or in the substrate. Many learn new habits in captivity – but some don't, especially if mouth position dictates feeding posture. Bottom-feeders may starve if offered floating food, or if all the food is eaten before any reaches the bottom; surface feeders, by contrast, may go hungry when sinking foods are given. Nocturnal feeders need to be fed after "lights out".

Food size is equally important. It should be small enough to be ingested and large enough to be worth the effort, but it does not end there. Don't expect a large lurking predator to chase around after small fry – it requires a single large prey item suited to its large mouth and hunting habits. A pursuit predator, by contrast, is often designed to capture smaller prey. Then again, a large mouth may denote a plankton feeder requiring small particles. More homework!

Notestes robustus, a brackish-water predator, polishing off a live fish. If you find the sight distasteful, obligatory piscivores are not for you.

You must consider whether your sensibilities will allow you to keep species that will eat only live prey, particularly live fishes. Don't try to convince yourself they will learn otherwise when they get hungry; if thousands of years of evolution have conditioned a fish to react only to live prey, it simply won't recognize anything else as food. It may perhaps learn eventually that anything you put into the tank is food, but then again it may not. It will certainly need live prey initially. So *never* buy a fish unless you can reconcile your conscience to feeding it what it needs.

While what to feed is largely a case of homework, how much is another matter, to be learned only by observing your particular mix of fishes. "As much as is eaten in five minutes" is an oft-quoted formula – all very well, but how much is that the first time you do it? The trick is to keep giving small amounts until interest wanes; and always siphon off uneaten food after every meal unless you have scavengers who will clear it up, in which case you must use your own judgement as to how much to leave.

How often should you feed? Well, that depends. If you have a piscivore which in nature eats one fish half its own size every other day, feed it that often. Fishes which feed continuously benefit from several small meals per day. Juveniles grow faster if fed more, and seasonal breeders need more to bring them into spawning condition. On the other hand, coldwater fishes kept in outdoor ponds shouldn't be fed at all during the colder months when they are inactive. Most aquarists overfeed, if only because feeding evokes a response from their pets. Perpetually bloated bellies, however, (except in gravid females) are as much a sign of ill-treatment as hollow ones.

The following are some of the different types of foods that can be used:

Dried Foods

There is no denying that dried foods such as flakes and pellets can, used sensibly, be a useful basis for the diet of many aquarium fishes, ensuring all the necessary proteins, vitamins, trace elements, and so on. There is an enormous choice available, and initially the best course is to buy the type which your fishes have been fed previously. Be aware of the dangers – apart from boredom – of using dried foods alone: unlike live foods they contain no coarse roughage, and fishes fed only on dried foods (especially by over-generous owners) often suffer digestive troubles and/or constipation, which can easily be fatal. Dried foods swell when thoroughly moistened, with potentially disastrous consequences if, as sometimes happens with greedy individuals, this takes place in the stomach. Avoid this by feeding sparingly when appropriate.

DRIED FOODS

Dried foods come in many varieties with different shapes, colours, and sizes: this is just a tiny selection of the different pellets and flakes available.

Koi pellets

Floating food hoops

Wheatgerm sticks

Spirulina flakes

Floating red pellets

Carnivore flake

Plant diet

Floating green pellets

Basic tropical flake

Goldfish food

Pond Foods

Most fishes relish anything that can be found swimming or crawling around in a pond (though for reasons of conservation do not feed them frogs, toads, newts, or their tadpoles). The most commonly used pond foods are *Daphnia* (water fleas) and bloodworm (midge larvae), both available commercially. Others – for example *Bosmina*, *Cyclops*, mosquito larvae, and, for larger fishes, water boatmen – you will normally have to catch for yourself. Some aquarists prefer not to use such foods for fear of introducing diseases and/or parasites, but this is highly unlikely, as ponds containing fishes (the source of diseases and parasites) tend not to have populations of live foods worth collecting! Do beware of predators such as dragonfly larvae and *Dytiscus marginalis* (the great diving beetle), which will eat small fishes and damage larger ones. Pond foods can be an essential element in conditioning breeding stock, and contain beneficial amounts of roughage. Many are now available frozen or freeze-dried (fishes appear to prefer the former).

Pond foods are much enjoyed by most fishes, and are excellent conditioning foods. *Daphnia* (water fleas) (*below*) are common in duck ponds, as are mosquito larvae (*bottom*), which can also be found in smaller bodies of water such as cattle troughs.

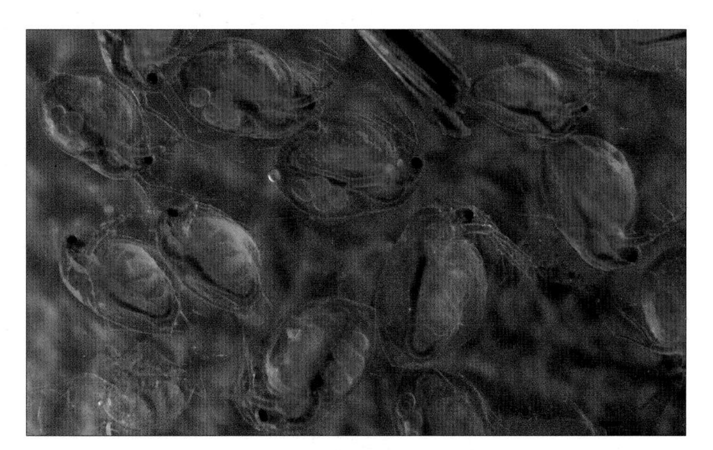

Other Live Foods

Earthworms, enjoyed by many fishes, can be fed whole or chopped to suit mouth size. Woodlice (collected) and crickets (bought) are suitable for larger mouths.

Whiteworms and grindal worms are small worms cultured in boxes of loamy soil. Starter kits can be obtained from dealers or by mail order. But feed only in small quantities as they can be fattening and constipating.

Tubifex are small red worms which live in mud (often around sewage outfalls) and are available from dealers. Always wash them before use. Although fishes enjoy them, you use them at your own risk, as their habitat makes them likely carriers of disease. Frozen or freeze-dried *Tubifex* are considered safe.

Before feeding to fishes, earthworms should be rinsed under the tap, or in a bucket of water, to remove any soil particles.

Culturing Whiteworms

1 Whiteworms can be cultured in a wooden or plastic box – large plastic food containers are ideal. Lay moist bread for the worms on the surface of the culture and cover with a piece of glass or perspex.

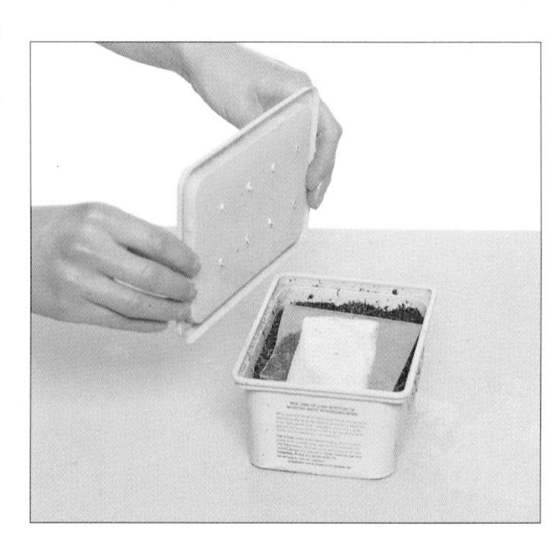

2 Keep the culture in darkness, but punch holes in the lid to allow for ventilation.

Artemia (brine shrimp) nauplii can be hatched from eggs for feeding fry; adults can be purchased for larger fishes. They should be rinsed in fresh water before use, to remove salt residues.

Live fishes used as foods are usually surplus fry, deformed or damaged (*never* diseased) specimens, or cheap, readily available aquarium fishes (often livebearers and goldfish). There is always a chance of introducing disease, so this diet should be used only where essential; never use wild native fishes.

Hatching Artemia *(brine shrimp)*

Brine shrimp are usually hatched in clear, preferably glass, containers (such as large bottles) filled with salt solution, which should be made up according to the instructions accompanying the eggs. (In the absence of any instructions, use 25 g (1 oz) of marine or cooking salt per litre (2 pints) of water.)

The containers should be stood in a warm place 18-24 °C (65-75 °F) and strongly aerated so that the eggs do not settle (if they "clog" on the bottom, the hatch rate will be greatly reduced).

When the eggs hatch, usually after 2-3 days, the nauplii (baby shrimps) can be harvested. Turn the aeration off and stand a light next to the container so that an area halfway up one side is brightly lit. The shrimps will be attracted to the light and can be siphoned off (using airline tube) relatively free of unhatched eggs and empty shells, which tend to sink to the bottom or float on the surface. Strain the shrimps through a fine net (to avoid adding salt to the aquarium).

Always remember to turn the aeration system back on.

Cultures will remain active for only a few days, so 3 should be started at 2 day intervals to ensure a succession of shrimps. Each can then be restarted from scratch on its 7th day, for as long as required.

Frozen and Freeze-dried Foods

These are available from most dealers, and represent a safe and convenient way of feeding pond and other natural foods. Frozen foods are, however, expensive and have a high water content, while freeze-dried ones are not always enjoyed, at least not at first.

Frozen and freeze-dried foods

Frozen (*left*) and freeze dried (*right*) foods are a safe and convenient way of feeding "live" foods. Frozen foods come in bubble-packed blocks or in plastic envelopes; small organisms such as *Tubifex* and bloodworm are usually freeze-dried in cubes (*top right*), while larger ones, such as river shrimp, are processed singly (*bottom right*).

Human Foods

A number of excellent foods can be "borrowed" from the kitchen – ox heart, liver, prawns and shrimps, mussels and other shellfish, cooked chicken, raw and cooked fish, and cod roe for carnivores; cucumber, courgette, peas, lettuce, and spinach for herbivores. Beware of feeding too much mammalian protein, which can cause digestive upsets and fatty degeneration of the tissues.

A selection of human foods suitable for various fishes. As long as additives are avoided, the only real limitation is your imagination.

Last, but not least, always regard feeding time as an opportunity to observe your fishes: to make sure they are all present and healthy, and that they are all getting their share.

Equipment

Preliminary visits to local retailers will probably leave you aghast at the sheer quantity and variety of equipment available – and its cost! Let us reassure you that you don't need to buy every available gadget and gizmo – no amount of expenditure on hi-tech equipment can buy success. Instead, supplement basic equipment with effort and observation. If you have doubts, remember that committed aquarists with multiple tanks could never afford all those gadgets for every one, yet they have healthy fishes and more fry than they know what to do with.

We have listed the items you need to get started, but the variety of different types available means you must make your own decisions about which kind to buy. Don't be afraid to ask your dealer for his opinion, or your hobbyist friends what they use, what they think of its reliability and convenience, and what they have to suggest by way of DIY.

The Tank

Obviously the first requirement is a tank. These are no longer made by fixing glass into an iron frame; instead sheets of glass are stuck together with silicon sealant, a by-product of the American space programme. This has made possible some interesting tank shapes, though they are not all as practical

Above: *Betta splendens* (Siamese fighting fishes) can be kept in small tanks as they can breathe atmospheric air. They should, however, have sufficient swimming space.

Right: Some fishes may jump during the dash to feed at the surface, and a hood and cover glasses are essential to keep them in.

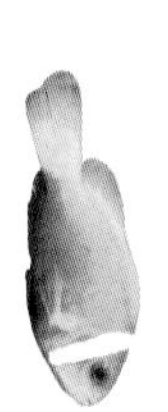

Check that the tank has bracing bars along the top edge of the long sides. Tanks more than 40 cm (15 inches) wide will normally have bracing along the short sides as well, and those more than 1 metre (36 inches) long a central glass "strap" from front to back.

as the traditional rectangular box in terms of surface area and accommodating equipment. Acrylic tanks are also available, but scratch easily. There are branded glass tanks which usually have a trim concealing some of the joins, but your dealer may make his own (or have a local supplier) at a far lower price. You must decide whether the plastic trim is worth the extra! Always check that tanks are made from new glass of a thickness appropriate to their size, and that the upper edges have reinforcing bars and, for tanks of 100 cm (3 ft) or more in length, a cross-bar to prevent water pressure bowing the long sides. *Never* use this to lift the tank – always lift from beneath.

Tank Sizes

Metric tank sizes differ from imperial tanks i.e. the metric tanks are not the exact equivalent size of the imperial tank. The table below lists both metric and imperial standard tank sizes. These sizes have been quoted throughout this book.

Metric	Imperial
50 x 25 x 25 (cm)	18 x 10 x 10 (inches)
50 x 30 x 30	18 x 12 x 12
60 x 30 x 30	24 x 12 x 12
100 x 40 x 40	36 x 15 x 15
120 x 40 x 40	48 x 15 x 15
150 x 50 x 50	60 x 18 x 18
180 x 60 x 60	72 x 24 x 24

The Stand

Next you need something on which to stand your aquarium; this must be flat and level, and capable of carrying the load involved. The most expensive unit is the purpose-built cabinet, which usually includes an aquarium and has a cupboard underneath for equipment and storage. Alternatively, there are welded metal stands, or you can make your own from bolted angle or treated timber, but seek expert advice. You may have a suitable solid surface in your home. Unless you are using a purpose-built cabinet you will need to buy a piece of exterior-grade plywood the size of the tank bottom and at least 15 mm (5/8 inch) thick; and between this and the tank it is essential to have a 13 mm (1/2 inch) thick (minimum) sheet of expanded polystyrene. These can be obtained from a hardware store, and are needed respectively to distribute the load and cushion the tank against any unevenness.

The Hood

The next essential is something to keep the fishes in the tank, minimize water loss by evaporation, and exclude intruders (furry pets, children, and dirt). The most basic option is to obtain from a glass merchant one or more pieces of glass (cover glasses) cut so as to fit on the glass struts inside the tank. A proper hood, however, offers more protection against intruders, keeps wiring tidy, and accommodates lighting. Hoods can be purchased or made, but in the latter case remember that the materials and construction must be such that there is no danger of contamination. Those used for marine aquaria must be resistant to salt corrosion.

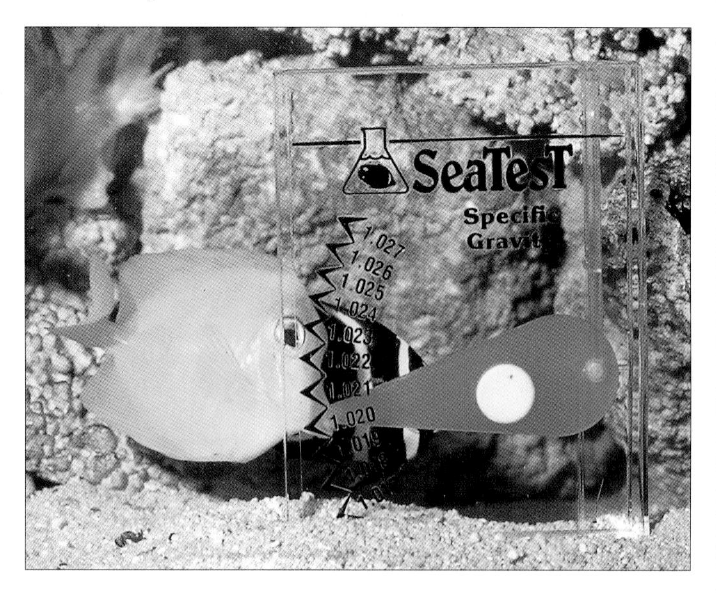

A hydrometer is essential if you intend keeping marines.

Heating

Unless you intend keeping coldwater fishes you will need equipment to maintain your tank at the right temperature. There are a number of options, and you must choose the one which best suits your needs. The most commonly used type is the combined immersion (internal) heater/thermostat; one problem with these, however, is that the thermostat usually lasts far longer than the heater element, so you may find yourself throwing away 50 per cent of your outlay unnecessarily at regular intervals. Separate thermostats, both internal and external, are also available, as are internal heaters and heating mats which go under the tank; remember, however, that if the latter type goes wrong you will be faced with either breaking down the tank to replace it, or using an internal heater instead.

Most thermostats are mechanical, operated by a conventional bimetallic strip opening and closing a set of electric contacts; the external type has to contact the tank side in order to sense the water temperature through the glass. Unfortunately these are sometimes affected by room temperature if this fluctuates significantly. Nowadays some external "stats" are electronic, with a sensor in the tank, but these are much more expensive and not necessarily more reliable. External stats are easier to adjust than internal ones – but beware of unauthorized adjustments by children!

The wattage of heating required depends on tank volume and ambient room temperature. Bear in mind that what suffices in summer may not be adequate at 3 am on a winter's night when the central heating is off. We suggest 50 watts per 30 litres (7 gallons) of aquarium water as a useful starting point, but try to err on the generous side rather

Filters range from the very basic (and cheap) internal box filter to highly sophisticated motorized units.

than risk chilling. The wattage of a heater makes little difference to its price, and a high wattage will heat the tank more quickly than a low one, costing the same but avoiding undue wear-and-tear on the heater(s).

Ideally, spread your eggs between two baskets and your wattage between two heater/stats: then if you don't notice that one heater element has failed, there will still be some heating; and if a thermostat jams on (more common than off) there is less chance of overheating.

Filtration and Aeration

Unless you are planning a heavily planted, low-population tank you will need a filter, and, for the marine aquarium, a protein skimmer. We have already discussed the various types on pages 29-31. Remember that filter volume and turnover rate should relate to aquarium volume, size and

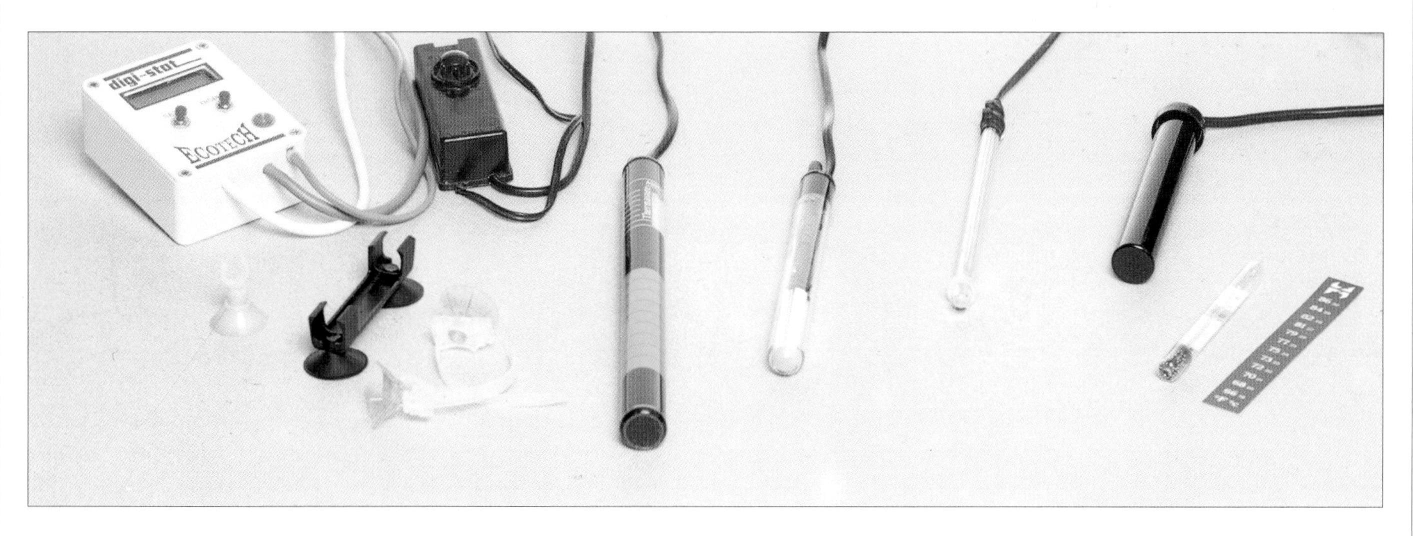

A selection of heating equipment.

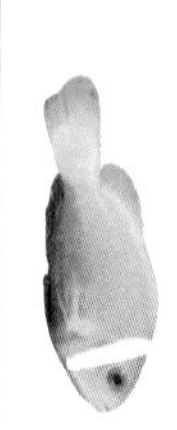

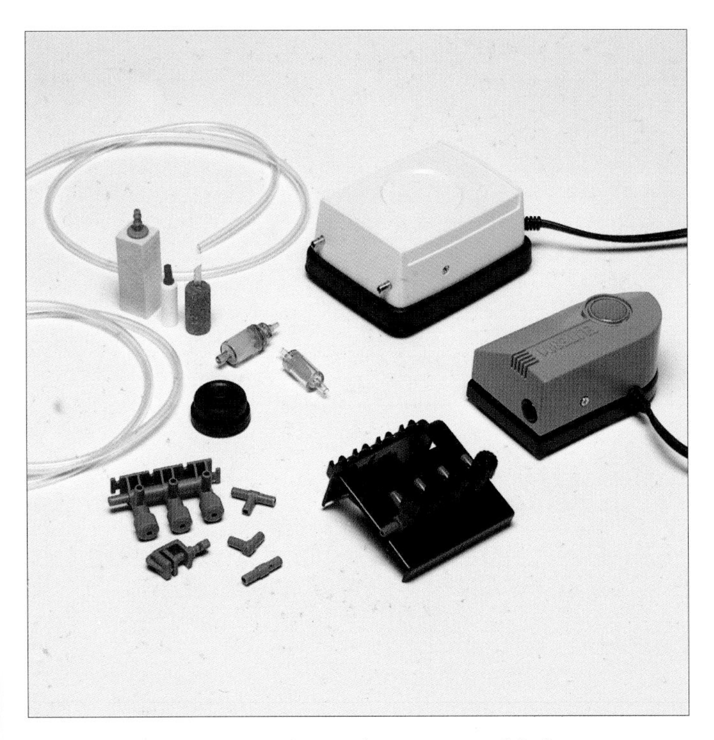

When selecting an air pump discuss your likely air requirement with your dealer before choosing a model of suitable capacity. Remember it is better to have too much rather than too little air. You will also need airline, a non-return valve for each pump outlet, and possibly some of the other accessories shown here.

number of fishes (and their appetites), and their preferences regarding water movement. If your tank is reasonably large it is worth considering having two small- or medium-sized filters instead of a single large one: their separate inlets can be better positioned to maximize waste intake; they can be cleaned out alternately to avoid loss of biological filtration; and if one breaks down there is still the other . . .

Don't forget to buy a supply of suitable filter media. Although there are various hi-tech types available (at a price), we suggest you use inexpensive media such as floss or foam in the first instance; alternatively aquarium gravel (coral sand for marine aquaria) makes an excellent medium (not just for UG filters).

Even if you do not expect to need additional aeration, and your filtration is power- rather than air-driven, we suggest you give consideration to the purchase of an airpump and some airline, if not at this stage, as soon as your pocket has recovered from the initial outlay. You may need it to operate a box filter or provide an air supply in a quarantine or hospital tank, to aerate brine shrimp hatcheries, to drive off chlorine from tap water, and for a thousand and one other uses.

Lighting

Although fishes generally look their best in natural light, it is difficult to arrange enough of this in the house to provide the average 12 hours per day needed by fishes and plants, and for a large part of the year it is not available in the evening - which may be the only time you are at home to enjoy your aquarium. Consequently you will require artificial lighting even if your tank receives some natural light. The most commonly used type is one or more fluorescent tubes inside the hood, controlled by a special choke unit. Use only chokes specifically designed for aquarium use – the ordinary domestic types lack certain safety features needed where water is involved. Chokes are designed to operate one or two tubes of the same wattage; unfortunately a 15 watt choke won't operate a 40 watt tube, so you must consider the likely amount of lighting required in advance. Tubes come in standard lengths/wattages, normal practice being to use a tube rather shorter than the aquarium, for example 60 cm (24 inches) tube (20 watts) for an 80 or 100 cm (30 or 36 inch) tank, and a 100 cm (36 inch) tube (30 watts) for a 110 or 120 cm (42 or 48 inch) tank. In tanks up to 40 cm (15 inches) wide and deep this will generally be sufficient for reasonable plant growth if a white light is used, and perfectly adequate for viewing the fishes. If you want to grow plants in deeper tanks, then give consideration to having two or more tubes to increase the amount of light penetrating to the bottom. Bear in mind, however, that this also increases the light in the upper layers, possibly to the discomfort of fishes from shady forest waters – if the lighting is too bright they may retaliate by hiding, although this can be overcome with a few floating plants. Marine aquaria are usually more brightly lit, this being necessary to encourage the unicellular algae needed as food by some invertebrates.

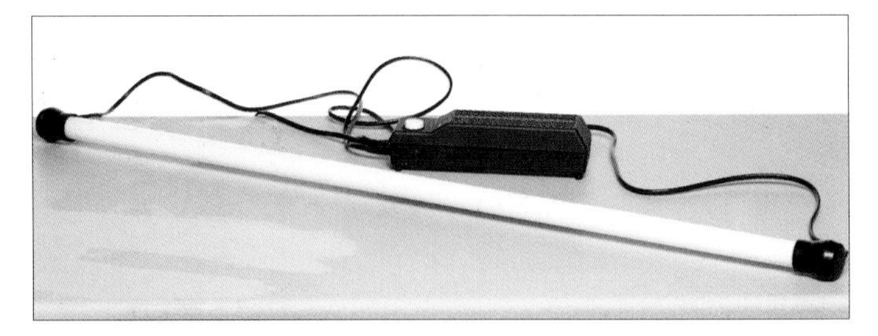

Special damp-resistant control units and tube leads are used for aquarium fluorescent lights; a variety of special tubes, which produce light in different areas of the spectrum, is available from good aquatic dealers, but ordinary domestic tubes can also be used.

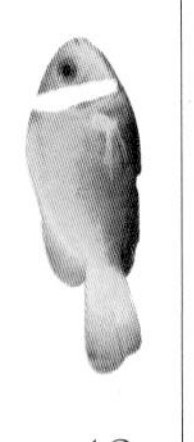

Recent years have seen the development of spotlights for aquarium use, and these can provide a very attractive light and shade effect, allowing light to be concentrated where needed without over-illuminating the entire aquarium. Unfortunately they cannot be accommodated inside the standard aquarium hood, and also work rather better without cover glasses. Use only spotlights designed for aquarium use.

Tubes and spotlights come in a variety of types producing light in different areas of the spectrum. Those near the blue end favour plant growth, but don't necessarily optimize fish colours. Lights with a high ultra-violet output can be harmful to human eyesight and should be screened from direct view. Ask your dealer to show you different tubes in action and then decide on the basis of your personal needs and preferences.

Ancillary Equipment

You will need a variety of testing equipment. First a thermometer for monitoring temperature; two types are available – stick-on external liquid crystal displays, and conventional alcohol or mercury thermometers which are fixed to the inside of the glass with a sucker. Both are frequently of dubious accuracy; the glass type can be calibrated by taking your temperature (37°C, 98.6°F) and noting the degree of inaccuracy. You will also need test kits – ammonia, nitrite, nitrate, pH, and hardness – and, for marines, a hydrometer for measuring salinity.

Don't forget any items needed to adjust your tap water chemistry and quality, as previously discussed; salt for marines; peat for lowering pH; coral sand as an alkaline buffer; something to remove nitrates; and, for creating soft water in a hard-water district, a reverse-osmosis unit, an ion-exchange softener, or a water butt for rainwater.

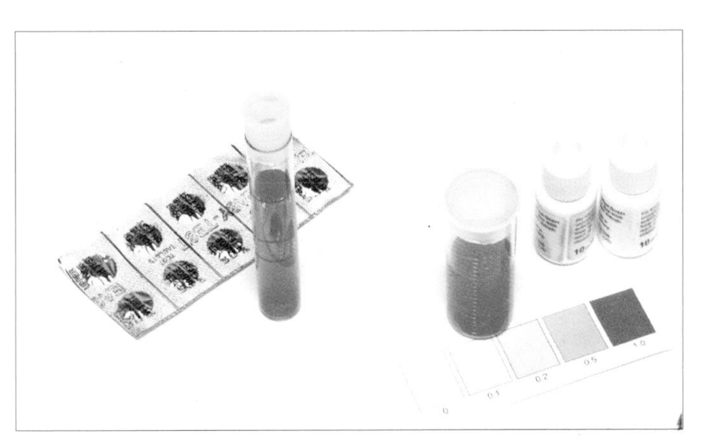

There are various test kits available on the market for testing the quality of your water, and they are all quick and simple to use.

Remember that all equipment for the marine aquarium must be non-metallic.

Finally, various bits and pieces: two nets of appropriate size, in case you need to catch a fish; a siphon/gravel cleaner; at least one plastic bucket; and, if you need to store water, one or more plastic bins. Use only plastic items designed for aquarium use or human foods (home brewing bins are ideal): white or clear plastic is usually safe.

New or Secondhand?

On adding up the cost of these basics you may be tempted to consider secondhand equipment, but be aware of the potential problems: used equipment may carry disease; tanks may be scratched, electrical equipment defunct, near the end of its lifespan, or unsafe – and you have no guarantees or other comeback. Ideally see equipment working before buying. "Complete set-ups" at knockdown prices can be tempting, but usually include fishes – do you really want someone else's choice, and are you capable of moving an aquarium and reinstalling its occupants in a matter of hours? If you must buy secondhand it is better to do so from your dealer, who may sometimes have suitable equipment, with, because he values your custom, some sort of guarantee.

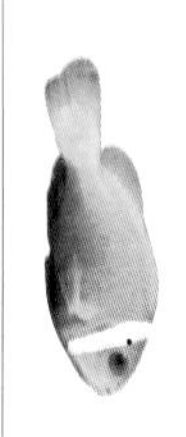

Decor – the hardware

Aquarium decor is not just a matter of creating a beautiful underwater landscape to please the onlooker: it also provides shelter and shade for the fishes, as well as a means of hiding unsightly equipment. It can be roughly divided into three sections: background, substrate, and interior decor proper. In this chapter we deal with the "hardware", while the "software" – that is to say, plants – is covered in the next chapter.

The prime consideration when choosing decor must be the requirements of the fishes. It should not be harmful (causing unintentional alteration of water chemistry, or worse, poisoning by unsuitable materials), and it must satisfy their psychological needs; there is no point in providing plants for fishes from rocky biotopes, or vice versa.

Above: When constructing your imitation reef, whether from coral, tufa, or other rocks, remember to leave plenty of holes and crevices as refuges for small fishes.

Right: Hardware can mean rocks or bogwood in a planted tank, but to many aquarists it conjures up something more dramatic, such as this Rift Valley cichlid aquarium.

Background

Remember that fishes of suitable size for aquaria are often several stages down the food chain, so their natural preference is not for wide open spaces but for the proximity of shelter, often at the edge of their biotope. You must, of course, provide them with shelter that they can actually utilize (caves, plants), but it is also important to offer them the security afforded by a background representing the edge of the river, lake, or pool – generally a bank with exposed tree roots, a rock face, or perhaps a reed bed. The marine equivalent is a rock face or coral reef.

Few aquarists give sufficient, if any, consideration (other than aesthetic) to the essential matter of background, and we have considerable misgivings about freestanding tanks that lack even the basic reassurance of a wall behind. It is in the aquarist's own interests to provide security at the back of the tank (and perhaps the ends as well), for if fishes feel secure they will parade confidently around the tank. Otherwise they may be nervous and hide much of the time; deprive them of hiding-places to prevent this and they will respond by cowering in corners.

Backgrounds can be external or internal, though in the latter case they must, of course, also be non-toxic and not have any adverse effects on water chemistry. Internal backgrounds prevent any mirror effect from the glass, an important factor when it comes to photographing your fishes – many a photo has been ruined by reflections in the back glass. Roofing slates (real, not synthetic) can be stood and/or glued against the back glass, or slivers of rock can be stuck to it using silicon sealant. Cork tiles (the plain type, without backing) can represent an earth bank in rainforest biotopes. Coral gravel can be used to simulate the side of the reef. For those with the time and inclination, styrofoam can be sculpted, or fibreglass moulded, to appropriate shapes, then painted in natural colours (non-toxic). Obviously the background should be appropriate to the natural habitat of the intended occupants, and the rest of the decor should be an extension of it.

This type of background can also be used externally, or there are a number of simpler alternatives. The outside of the glass can be painted a plain colour; dark blue or green is often used for marine tanks ("the sea"), black or dark brown ("earth" or "rock") for freshwater. Even though a plain background of this sort is not entirely natural, it provides a solid and unobtrusive backdrop to the rest of the underwater scene. Light colours, by contrast, may dominate; they can hardly be said to simulate the security of the riverbank, and, while perhaps initially attractive to the human eye, the novelty soon wears off. Bear in mind that once paint has been applied it may be difficult to remove if you change your mind.

An alternative is to glue coloured paper or plastic sheeting (the above suggestions on colours apply equally here) to the outside of the glass. Although paper is cheaper, it is vulnerable to damp, and difficult to keep in place without the liberal use of glue – just as difficult to remove as paint, and visible through the glass. Plastic can be secured by spots of glue along top and bottom edges, where it won't show. Most dealers stock rolls of background, for sale in appropriate lengths. These are waterproof, but, like paper, flexible and thus difficult to keep in place. They depict underwater scenery, and in our view are horribly artificial when combined with the real thing. They are, however, much better than no background at all. There is no real restriction on what you use externally, provided you remember that it should offer security and be either unobtrusive or a match for the rest of the decor. Stained chipboard or plain dark carpet are two further possibilities.

Above: **A selection of background materials. *Clockwise from bottom left:* slate, styrofoam, cork tiles, freshwater and marine "background on a roll".**

Right: **Cichlids can be prevented from digging by using a pebble substrate, though it is unkind to thus inhibit their natural behaviour. Some cichlids may improvise bizarre spawning "pits" as these mouthbrooders have done with an empty shell.**

Substrate

A substrate is essential, not just because the aquarium looks unfinished without it, but because fishes do not live over bare glass in nature, and prefer a natural base to their world. It provides an anchoring medium for plants and other decor, and, even if UG filters are not used, a home for essential nitrogen cycle bacteria.

In freshwater aquaria the substrate is usually gravel or sand, while for marines coral sand (or coral gravel) is the norm, providing not only a natural setting (most tropical aquarium marines are coral fishes), but also an ever-present pH buffer. Unfortunately this buffering capacity has led to the use of coral sand for freshwater fishes from alkaline waters, and, by extension, occasionally for other freshwater species, regardless of their requirements. Although small amounts can be mixed with gravel as a pH buffer where appropriate, coral sand should otherwise be regarded as unsuitable for freshwater aquaria; its light colour leads to glare, resulting in timid and poorly coloured fishes, and its use can also produce outbreaks of scratching, apparently gill irritation caused by tiny particles suspended in the water.

Opposite: **Small coral fishes such as this *Pomacentrus coeruleus* (electric blue damsel) find refuge from predators in crannies in the coral reef. Similar hiding places are appreciated in captivity.**

Below: **Some Lake Tanganyika cichlids live in shells, and it is cruel to keep them without this type of shelter.**

Some killifishes, such as these *Aphyosemion sjoestedti* (blue gularis), require a substrate of loose peat to spawn in.

SUBSTRATE MATERIALS

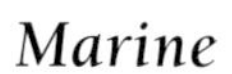

Freshwater

Various different types of gravel are available for the freshwater aquarium. *Top*: black gravel is ideal for fishes from shady habitats. *Above left*: "ordinary" aquarium gravel. *Above right*: ungraded granite gravel – this is "hardness free" and thus suitable for soft-water set-ups. The varied grain size creates a more natural effect than with graded types.

Marine

Coral sand (*top*), and limestone chips (*above*) are suitable substrates for the marine aquarium. The latter can also be used in hard freshwater set-ups, but the use of coral sand for such aquaria is not recommended.

Gravel, like water, is of variable composition. It comes in various grain sizes and varying degrees of sharpness, not to mention different colours. Much aquarium gravel contains calciferous material which will increase hardness and pH, so for soft acid water aquaria you must track down some "hardness-free" sand or gravel. Remember that in shady forest streams the bottom is often covered with leaf litter, so fishes from such waters may prefer a darker substrate. Some fishes dig as part of their feeding or breeding procedure, and will have problems if the grains are too large for their mouths. Those which sift substrate through their gills when feeding may be harmed by large or sharp-edged grains. Fine sand clogs easily, and is not ideal for UG filtration. All these factors must be considered before making a final decision.

If you are using UG filtration a substrate 6.5–7.5 cm (2½–3 inches) thick is needed; otherwise about 4–5 cm (1½–2 inches) is sufficient. A 25 kg (56 lb) bag of gravel will provide roughly a 2.5 cm (1 inch) layer in a 100x40 cm (36x15 inch) tank. Some fishes are avid diggers, and this has led to the invention of the "gravel tidy", buried in the substrate to limit excavation. Remember it is unkind to prevent instinctive behaviour, and position any tidy so that some digging is possible. Gravel tidies can also cause problems with planting and with "bedding" rocks in place, so consider carefully whether you really need one.

Acanthophthalmus sp. (the Kuhli loach, _bottom left_) likes to burrow in the substrate, which should be of fine sand. The only problem for the aquarist, however, is that it may make them impossible to catch.

Interior decor

Here again all materials must be non-toxic, must not have any adverse effect on water chemistry, and be appropriate to the natural requirements of the fishes. For marines the usual materials are rocks and dead corals, and, for those prepared to satisfy its stringent requirements, "living rock" (live corals, molluscs, crustaceans and so on). The rock sold for use with marines is tufa, a highly porous, and thus lightweight, limestone which can be piled up into impressive structures. There is, however, no reason why other types of rock shouldn't be used provided they don't adversely affect water chemistry and contain no veins of metals or other toxic contaminants.

Right: **Concern about damage to coral reefs has led to the manufacture of artificial corals for aquarium use. Once they have developed a coating of algae they look quite natural.**

Bogwood provides shelter, resting places and nutrient for some fishes such as *Panaque nigrolineatus* (royal plec).

A selection of rocks suitable for aquarium use

Clockwise from right: Slate, sandstone, red granite, limestone, mica schist, banded gneiss. Limestone is suitable only for hard and salt water set-ups. Water-worn rocks, such as the red granite shown here, give a more natural effect.

The same applies to rocks for freshwater tanks. Tufa is popular for fishes from rocky habitats, but should be used (as should any calciferous rock) only for hard-water biotopes. A point not often realized is that it is too rough for use as a spawning substrate by many species which lay their eggs on a rock surface. Other rocks which may be suitable are granites, schists, slates, sandstones, gneisses, and many more. Rock is sold by weight and is not cheap, so you may be tempted to collect your own – but don't do so unless you are able to identify different types of rocks and spot any contaminants in them. Smooth water-worn pieces look more natural than jagged lumps.

Many cichlids, such as *Amphilophus citrinellus* (Midas cichlid), dig as part of their breeding behaviour. This behaviour can be prevented by covering the tank bottom with rocks and pebbles, but may in turn prevent successful breeding.

Rocky Shoreline (as for many East African lake set-ups)

1 Bed the foundation rocks firmly on the filter plate or tank bottom. Use large pieces whose weight will add to the stability of the structure.

2 Conceal flowerpots in bottom storey caves to help avoid substrate infilling from behind, deter unauthorized excavation, and provide an increased sense of security for the occupants.

3 Add the rest of the substrate, carefully infilling around the foundations with your fingertips, so that they are completely secure and safe.

4 Position the "roofing" slabs. Large pieces are often easier to fit securely and create a more stable structure.

5 Check that each superimposed rock fits tightly on the foundations. If necessary, experiment with different pieces until a good fit is obtained.

6 Continue to build up the rockwork, again checking the stability of each new piece, until the desired effect is achieved.

7 Bogwood is lighter than rock and useful for adding extra height (i.e. if you wanted to conceal any equipment) without overloading the structure.

8 Bogwood should be suitably "weathered" or varnished for alkaline water set-ups. The odd piece of "driftwood" is quite likely to occur in natural rocky settings.

Although this completed rocky decor looks bleak at this stage, the rocks will develop a coating of algae over time and thus a more mellow appearance.

The blind cave characin is the blind, albino, cave-dwelling form of a normally sighted species, *Astyanax mexicanus*.

Many catfishes, like cichlids, appreciate a cave for shelter. This is *Malapterurus electricus* (the electric catfish).

The amount of rock to be used will depend on the biotope you are trying to replicate, and may range from scattered stones on the floor of a forest stream to large and complex rockpiles representing an area of rapids or rocky lake shore. Stones can be used to support raised terraces of substrate material. Never position rocks on top of the substrate – always bed them in it so they cannot be undermined, either by substrate slippage or fish excavations. Always make sure rocky structures are solidly constructed so they cannot collapse, crushing fishes or crashing through the glass; consider sticking them together with silicon sealant for added security and stability.

Some fishes require caves as shelter and/or spawning areas, and these can, of course, be made from rocks. A popular alternative is to use clay flowerpots or drainpipes (which may, however, increase hardness and pH), or food-grade plastic pipe, which can be concealed under rocks or among plants. Always use new pots and pipes – old ones from the garden may be contaminated with pesticides or fertilizers. Resist the temptation to use shells as caves except for fishes which use them as shelter in nature – and then only in hard-water biotopes, as they contain calcium carbonate and will increase hardness and pH. Avoid ornate marine shells in freshwater aquaria as they look horribly out of place. The same goes for corals, which also increase hardness and pH.

Flowerpots and drainpipes make excellent "instant caves". It does not matter if they are broken!

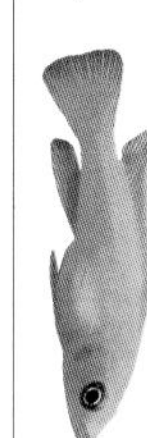

Rainforest biotope simulations benefit from the use of bogwood, coconut shells, and cork bark. All of these will tend to leach tannins into the water, acidifying it and turning it brown; even in acid-water aquaria this can be too much of a good thing, so new materials of this kind should be "aged" by soaking, or leaving them outside to weather. Coconut shells should be free of fibre and nut residues. These wooden items can be varnished for use in alkaline conditions, but check that none of your fishes has a taste for nibbling wood, as varnish is toxic if consumed. Wooden items have a disconcerting tendency to float until thoroughly waterlogged, and may need to be wedged into place with stones.

The materials discussed above are natural ones, but there are also a variety of "artefacts" available. These range from excellent simulations of wood, virtually indistinguishable from the real thing, to plastic mermaids and shipwrecks, which can hardly be said to benefit the fish or help provide a natural underwater scene! For those lacking green fingers, or who want greenery able to survive the attentions of herbivorous fishes, there are plastic versions of most popular aquarium plants. Again these range from the remarkably realistic to the unmitigatedly

Stream Bed with Cork Bark Logs and Plastic Plants

1 Cork bark can be used to conceal equipment such as a UG filter uplift. It can be prevented from floating by wedging the bottom end in the substrate and the top under the tank's bracing bars

2 Rocks can be used to prevent sideways slippage. As always they should be firmly bedded on the bottom, and large enough for the intended purpose.

3 A second piece of cork bark acts as an imitation log on the river bed. This time it must be weighted with slate attached to its underside, or with stones concealed inside.

4 Provided the water is added carefully, plastic plants can be added at the dry stage of setting up. As with living plants, groups of a single species often create a more natural effect.

5 The finished decor. Note there are spaces within the rocks and the cork bark, such as the "hollow log" for the fishes to use as hiding places. Algae will eventually grow on the rocks, wood and the plastic plants. While this may look realistic on the wood and rocks it should be removed from the plants by taking them out and scrubbing them.

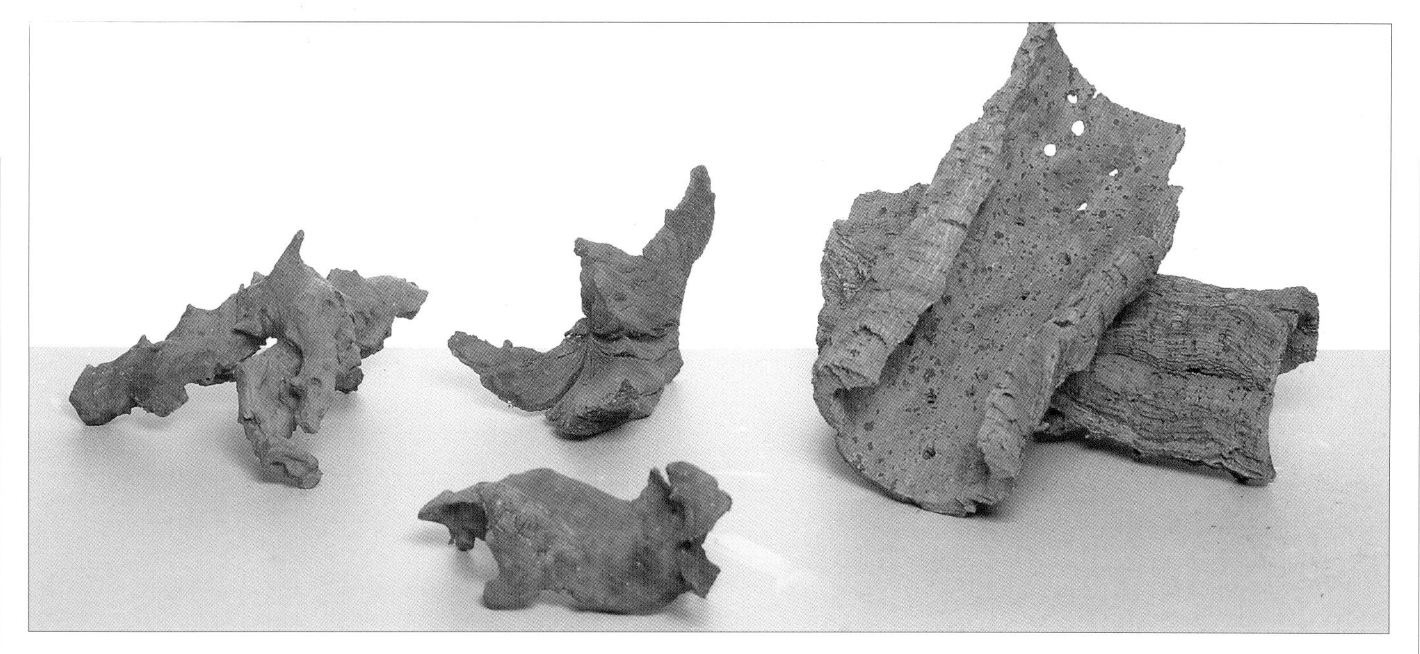

Cork bark (*right*) and bogwood (*centre*) require careful preparation before use. Artificial wood (*left*) can be extremely realistic, needs no treatment, and has the added advantage that, unlike real wood, it doesn't float!

awful; fishes don't appear to be aesthetically affected, so the choice is up to you.

Never forget that in choosing and arranging your decor you must always keep the fishes' requirements – water chemistry, shelter, swimming space, and so on – in mind, and be prepared to forego any ideas which may please your eye but cause them physical or psychological discomfort. Your aim should be to provide them with a replica of their natural environment in which they will feel at home. They will reward you by looking their best.

Julidochromis (this is *J. regani* 'Kipili') are obligatory rock-dwellers which rarely stray more than a few centimetres from rocks.

Uaru will nibble at bogwood, which should therefore never be varnished for use in their aquarium.

PLASTIC PLANTS

Ceratopteris thalictroides (Indian fern)

Ludwigia

Vallisneria

Ambulia

Some plastic plants – for example those at the top – are more realistic than the other examples below them. Greater realism can sometimes be achieved by positioning two plants together to create the effect of a single, larger, more vigorous plant.

Decor – plants

There is a great variety of plants offered for sale as aquatic plants. They fall into three categories: a) true aquatic plants, b) marginal plants and c) terrestrial plants, and it is important that you understand the difference between the three types. It is also wise to find out about the water conditions the plants like because, just as with your fishes, there are those that prefer hard, soft, acid, alkaline, or brackish water. Some will tolerate a wide range of conditions but there are others that have very specific requirements if they are to thrive, so it's homework time again.

True Aquatic Plants

These spend all their time submerged in water; so to remove them from it is to condemn them to death. They are usually sold as cuttings, and *Cabomba* is a prime example.

Marginal Plants

Marginals spend only part of the year submerged; during the dry season they grow out of water and most flower and seed at this time of year. The majority of our aquarium plants are from this group. Marginals may be sold as rooted plants, for example *Echinodorus* and *Cryptocoryne*, or they may be cuttings such as *Hygrophila*.

Above: **Marginal plants, and those which are submerged for only part of the year in nature, are best grown in the paludarium rather than the aquarium.**

Opposite: ***Trichogaster trichopterus*** **(three-spot gourami) with a dwarf tropical water lily.**

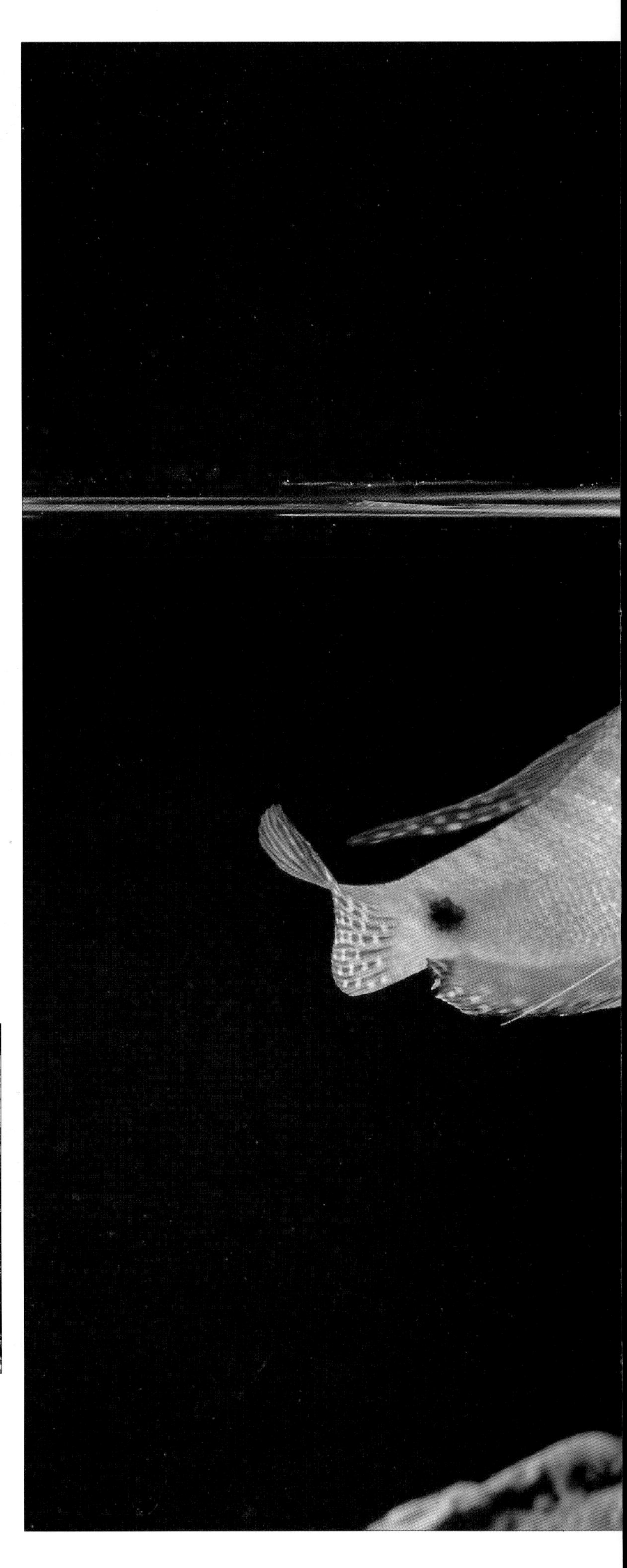

Caulerpa (*bottom of picture*), a kind of algae, is the only plant available for marine aquaria. Sea anemones (*top of picture*) are, of course, animals, not plants.

In the "Dutch aquarium" plants, rather than fishes, are the most important feature of the display.

Terrestrial Plants

As their name suggests, these grow out of water, and can survive without being submerged at all. Although they can live for up to three or four months underwater, they are not recommended for aquarium use. Indeed some of them, for example *Dieffenbachia* (dumb cane), have poisonous sap but are nevertheless still offered as aquarium plants.

Purchasing

We need to treat aquarium plants with as much respect as fishes. Some are tropical, and therefore need to be kept warm. It is important not to chill them when bringing them home or by planting them in cold water because, just as a tropical houseplant will shed its leaves when chilled or, worse, curl up and die, so will your aquatic plants. Avoid buying tropical plants from cold tanks (feel the glass) or from trays of cold water (dabble fingers). Some plants, for example *Vallisneria*, get "transparent" patches in the leaves if they've been chilled. So long as they are kept damp and warm, they need not be submerged in water to carry them home. The plants you purchase may be cuttings, which are just lengths of stem with leaves and a growing tip but no roots, or they may be individual rooted plants.

Before going to buy your plants you need to plan, on paper, the layout for the aquarium and the plants you think will be suitable for each area. Just as importantly, pick the plants that you like because it is you that has to live with the finished aquarium. Check up on the size they grow to and the colours and textures of the leaves, and try to combine the groups of plants so that they complement each other. Murphy's Law states that when you go to your dealer he won't have all the plants you've chosen, but that really doesn't matter because you can leave a gap and add the others at a later date, building the plant stocks as carefully as you build the fish stocks because, just as too much fish waste can cause a strain on a new filtration system, so can too many dead leaves.

Having bought your plants and got them home, the fun begins. Lay the plants out in shallow trays of warm water so that you can easily see what you have – roasting tins are ideal for this. Check the length of cuttings and, if they are too long, trim them to the right length before planting. Cut the stems with scissors rather than pinching them with your fingers so that you avoid bruising – any tissue damage leaves the plant open to disease.

Planting

The substrate used for plants must allow the free passage of their roots and free movement of water. A fine gravel or coarse sand is ideal.

Whatever plants you have chosen the planting methods will be basically the same. Treat them as you would a garden plant – after all, your aquarium is to be a miniature underwater garden. Just as you would never plant two rose bushes in the same hole and expect them both to grow to their full potential, so aquatic plants should never be planted in bunches. Space the plants so that light can penetrate to the substrate and thus the lower leaves are less likely to turn yellow and die back. The distance between the plants should be the span of their leaves, and to achieve the effect of a wall of plants when viewed from the front, place the plants in staggered rows.

Not all plants need to be planted; some float and others require attachment to rocks or wood. *Microsorium pteropus* (Java fern) may be tied on to wood or rock with fishing line and eventually its roots will anchor it in place. *Vesicularia dubayana* (Java moss) is often left free until it finds its own anchorage point. Once established it grows prolifically and needs frequent trimming back.

In general, tall plants should be sited at the rear of the aquarium and smaller ones at the front.

Cuttings

The main plants sold as cuttings are *Cabomba*, *Myriophyllum*, *Synnema*, *Rotala*, *Elodea*, and *Hygrophila*. Of these, the fine-leaved *Cabomba* is probably one of the most popular aquarium plants for beginners, though it is also one of the hardest to succeed with. Its bushy, ferny appearance makes it ideal for hiding filter pipes and heaters, but this all too often means that it is in the most turbulent areas of water. Its fronds are delicate and easily damaged, so it is best used in a quiet area of the aquarium. The many *Hygrophila* species are far better suited to hiding pipes, as their leaves and stems are more robust and able to cope with the flow of water. So, once again, it's a case of doing your homework and checking on exactly what your plants need to succeed. If they are not growing well in one area of the tank don't be afraid to move them, but bear in mind that they will often take several months to settle – so don't expect instant rapid growth.

These plants feed mainly through their leaves, using their fine roots just to anchor them in the substrate; indeed, many will grow equally well if left floating free in the water and are thus often used as a spawning medium and hiding place for the subsequent fry.

Sometimes the cuttings offered for sale are taken at a time when the plant is growing above water. The stems are hard and woody, sometimes with hairs on them, the leaves are quite tough, and, when you hold them at their base, they stand upright (those that have been grown underwater flop down as they need water to support them upright). These woody cuttings can be planted in the same way as others but be aware that all the leaves will die off and you will be left with just bare stems. Be patient. Shoots should appear from the leaf joints and as they grow you will notice that their stems are soft and their leaves may be a totally different shape and colour from the emersed leaves of the original cuttings. When they are long enough, cut off the shoots and plant as you would any other cutting – it is this underwater growth that you now need to propagate, planting each cutting individually and spacing the young plants so that light can reach the bottom leaves. What you have done is re-create the rainy season when the floods come and submerge the plants, thus encouraging them to grow in their submerged form.

Plants such as *Cabomba* can be propagated by cutting off the top section and planting it. The rooted bottom section can be left *in situ* or replanted.

***Microsorium pteropus* (Java fern) is a very hardy plant which will withstand low light levels and attacks by herbivores, and can be grown on the hard decor if digging is likely to be a problem.**

Rooted Plants

Rooted plants require a little more effort. Depending on the size of your aquarium, choose them with care. Some of the *Echinodorus* species (Amazon swordplants) can grow large – right out of the water in fact – but there are some which are manageable, notably *E. paniculatus*, which makes a nice specimen plant for the average-sized aquarium, and *E. tenellus*, (the pygmy chain sword), an ideal plant for the foreground as it will quickly carpet the substrate.

Cryptocoryne species are other favourites. Although they are slow growers and take time to establish themselves, once settled they will grow into attractive clumps of plants which will eventually need thinning out to maintain their vigour. Again, choose your plants with care as they come in many sizes and leaf colours.

***Echinodorus* species (sword plants) are popular aquarium plants from South America. They require good light to thrive. In nature they have an emerse period during which they reproduce by flowering.**

Basket-grown Plants

These days many plants are offered as basket-grown specimens. These have been cultivated in nurseries, usually by mist propagation, whereby they are grown in very humid conditions. You have two choices as to how you plant these in your aquarium: you can either sink the complete basket in the substrate, in which case the plant roots will grow out through the holes in the basket into the gravel, or you can remove the plant from the basket. Personally we prefer to remove the plant and gently tease away the fibreglass growing medium from the roots. This is a time-consuming, painstaking job as you must try not to damage the roots. When buying *Cryptocoryne* plants you may find that what was purchased as one plant often turns out actually to be four or five smaller plants potted up as one. By planting them individually in the aquarium each will eventually grow into a good plant. One point of interest, and one of the main reasons for originally deciding to remove the plants from their growing medium, is that the fibreglass material is irritating to the fingers – what then might it do to bottom-dwelling fishes that rubbed against it? Some plants are grown in a papier-mâché-type medium: its drawback is that bits of it float around in the aquarium if fishes dig about in the basket. Another reason for removal of the baskets is that no matter how hard you try to conceal them, eventually they appear above the surface of the substrate, either excavated by fishes or because the sand/gravel has been moved by the flow of water in the tank.

Some pots actually contain several plants which should be planted separately. The *Cryptocoryne beckettii*, shown to the right, in fact consisted of the four smaller specimens seen below.

Some plants are sold in plastic pots, often containing rooting media which are "suspect" for use with fishes. If plants are to be grown in pots – for example to prevent disturbance by bottom-sifting fishes – they should be re-potted using gravel or sand, or compost topped with gravel, as the medium.

Below: This aquarium, with healthy plants of varying shapes and sizes – taken into account when designing the lay-out – is a pleasure to behold, as well as an ideal home for small, non-destructive fishes such as these tetras.

Above: Some plants, such as this *Anubias* species, have attractive coloured stems complementing the green of their foliage.

Bulbs and Corms

There are also various bulbs and corms that can be planted in the aquarium. Of these, *Aponogeton* and *Nymphaea* species are the best known. *Aponogeton* plants grow well, producing long, attractive leaves, and will even flower in the aquarium. If conditions are right, they may set seed which will eventually grow into new plants.

Nymphaea species are tropical water lilies and their one aim in life is to throw up lily pads and flower. This is fine if that is what you bought them for, but in your community aquarium such a lily would cover the whole of the tank surface, cutting out light to all your other plants. When these lilies start into growth, they produce a rosette of soft, pink to red underwater leaves which are very attractive. To maintain this lush underwater growth it is necessary to pinch out any leaf that heads for the surface. By doing this you will maintain the basal rosette but will never get any flowers: the choice is yours!

Below: Some dwarf tropical water lilies (*Nymphaea* species) are suitable for the aquarium, though they may shade/crowd out less vigorous plants. A large air-space above the water's surface is required for them to flower, and the blossoms are best viewed in an unhooded tank.

***Above:* Lemna minor (duckweed) is a pest to be avoided at all costs...**

***Below:* ...although it can be useful for deterring hatchet fishes such as *Carnegiella strigata* from jumping out of the water.**

Floating Plants

Floating plants are rarely used in community aquaria as they reduce the light reaching other plants, but, like Java moss, they are very useful as spawning sites and hiding places in breeding tanks. Those most commonly used are *Pistia stratiotes* (water lettuce), *Ceratopteris thalictroides* (Indian fern), and *Riccia*.

There is, however, one floating plant to avoid: *Lemna* (duckweed), which will quickly multiply to cover the water's surface, cutting out the light to other plants. It also clogs filters!

A few fishes will eat it, but prevention is the best course. Check all plants for duckweed before you put them in the aquarium, to avoid introducing even a single piece. If you do get an infestation then net out every offending piece, and avoid transferring this pest to other tanks on your nets.

Feeding

All the rooted plants, including *Aponogetons* and lilies, need feeding with pellets of proprietary fertilizer or clay to promote healthy growth, but don't overdo it: one or two pellets per plant every month or so, poked into the gravel within the root run, is fine. If you keep rabbits or guinea pigs, their droppings are an excellent fertilizer, and come ready pelleted! Dry and store in a tin, for use as above.

Although large cichlids (and some other fishes) are inimical to plants, most dwarf species are well-suited to, and require, a well-planted aquarium. This is *Microgeophagus ramirezi* (the ram or butterfly cichlid).

Lighting

Tropical plants require tropical lighting. In an ideal world they would get 12 hours of light and 12 of darkness, but as most people like to observe their fishes late into the evening the lights are usually on for longer than this. What many do require is more intense lighting than we would normally give them – the use of three 40w strip lights over a 120 x 50 cm (48 x 18 inch) aquarium works well. Use time switches so that they come on in sequence, ideally building up to a peak of intense light lasting for eight hours, and then go off in sequence, over a total lighting period of 12 hours. Lighting for plants must be compatible with the fishes' preferences; plants will reduce light by providing shade.

Some plants require more light than others – for example, some of the *Cryptocoryne* species require shady conditions, whereas water lilies require intense light if they are to maintain their pink or red colour. In this case plant the "Crypts" where they receive shade from a broad-leaved plant, and the lily in the open. It's just like gardening – if a plant needs shade you position it beneath a larger, broad-leaved plant.

Propagation

It is possible to propagate your plants. Some multiply readily, especially those, such as *Vallisneria* and many of the *Cryptocoryne* species, which throw out runners that root into the substrate, forming new plants. Other plants will grow from seed. Probably the easiest method for the beginner, however, is taking cuttings – you can venture into the more difficult realms of aquatic plant cultivation once you've gained some confidence in your ability to grow the easier types.

If your original cuttings are growing well and getting too tall, remove them and cut them to size, replacing the shortened top sections in the aquarium. The lower part of the stem can be planted in another tank and allowed to grow. Shoots that appear from the leaf joints can be nipped off when large enough and planted in the main tank.

Some of the *Rotala* and *Bacopa* species can be layered. Pin down the stem with a hairpin and within a few weeks shoots which can be used as new cuttings will appear from the leaf joints.

Other plants produce adventitious growths – small plantlets grow on the leaves. When these are large enough, they fall from the parent plant or can be removed and used as new plants. *Microsorium pteropus* (Java fern) and *Ceratopteris thalictroides* (Indian fern) use this method of reproduction.

Propagating *Microsorium pteropus* (Java fern)

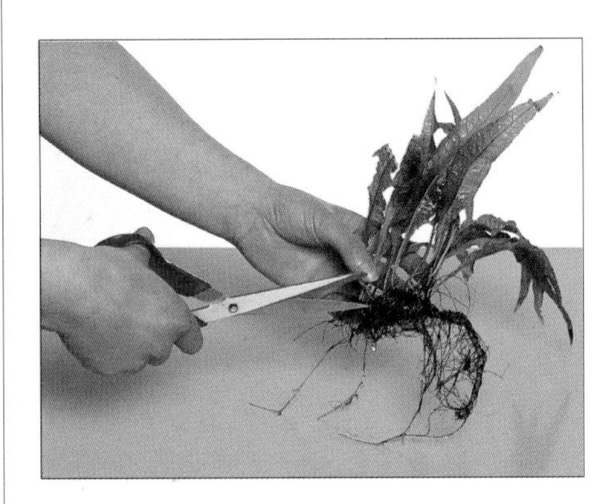

1 Java fern produces long woody stems with clinging roots which attach the plant to suitable surfaces on rocks, roots, and branches. Groups of leaves grow all along the stem, which can be severed...

2 ....to produce two or more separate plants. These extra plants can then be planted in the substrate, ensuring that the crown remains clear of the gravel.

3 It is, however, better to grow this plant on rocks or bogwood. Secure each plant with thread or a rubber band, which is removed once the roots have established a grip.

4 In addition damaged leaves, or those which have become detached, will produce adventitious plantlets (*left*), and by the time the parent leaf has rotted away these are usually large enough to survive independently. Sometimes a leaf will produce only one or two plantlets (*right*) which thus grow more quickly and may be ready for planting while the parent leaf remains.

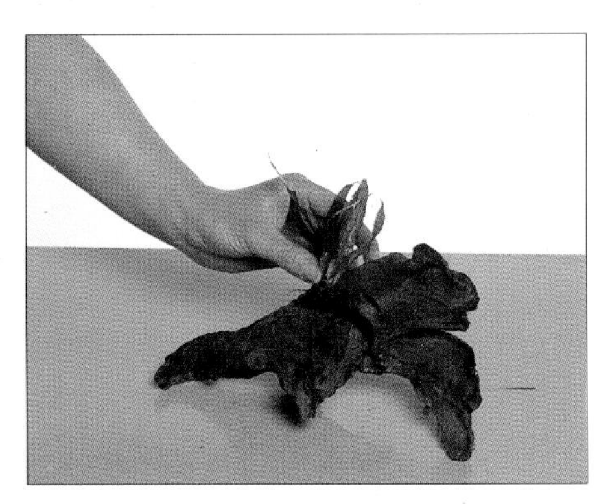

5 Secure the plantlets to a suitable surface as before. Alternatively the parent leaf, complete with plantlets, can be sited so that the plantlets can attach themselves naturally.

Algae

In the freshwater aquarium algae are considered a nuisance. No tank is ever completely free from them but they can be kept under control. When an aquarium is first set up with fresh water and new plants, it takes time for the latter to adapt to their new conditions, put out roots, and start to grow. Algae adapt far more quickly and an algal bloom occurs as they feed on the nutrients in the fresh water. At this stage the reaction of most people is to change the water and start again, but this will only aggravate matters as the new water will once again feed the algae.

As the higher plants begin to grow they feed on the nutrients and eventually outgrow the algae – you never get rid of all of it, but most of us think that a little bit of algae gives the aquarium a lived-in feel and some fishes certainly benefit from browsing on it. Various products are available to kill algae but they can be more trouble than they are worth. Unless all the dead algae are removed, they put a strain on the filtration system. It is far better to allow Nature to take its course and the tank to progress through the natural cycles. Achieving a fully planted aquarium with healthy fishes and plants takes time – months, in fact.

In the marine aquarium algae are of two types: unwanted and wanted. Beneficial algae, for example *Caulerpa* species, are grown to decorate the aquarium, while the unwanted algae are not really algae at all, nor are they bacteria, but belong to a class of their own, the Cynophycea. Commonly referred to as "blue-green algae" or "slime algae", they are often found when the water quality has deteriorated (even in freshwater tanks) as they are quick to utilize light and carbon dioxide to multiply, producing oxygen which can be seen as bubbles within the slime. During the maturation period, brown diatomaceous algae and hair algae may also be present but as conditions improve these algae should decrease. Attention to water quality is essential to prevent these unwanted algae from ruining your aquarium.

The beneficial algae may be purchased from your dealer. Buy as large a piece as you can afford as they can be difficult to establish. They attach themselves to rocks with a holdfast and "leaves" grow out from the runners. You should check on the fishes you intend to keep before purchasing the *Caulerpa,* in case they feed on algae.

As with the freshwater aquarium, successfully establishing these plants takes time and patience.

Vallisneria **species propagate naturally by runners, and will eventually carpet the substrate. Young plants can be removed – ideally not until they are 7.5 cm (3 inches) or more high – without uprooting the parent plant, and replanted elsewhere.** ***Vallisneria*** **should always be planted with their crowns just above the substrate; if the crown is buried the plant will not thrive.**

In sunlight, plants and algae (freshwater and marine) will produce visible bubbles of oxygen.

Pistia stratiotes **(water lettuce) is an attractive floating plant best suited to open-topped aquaria or indoor pools.**

Setting Up

Setting up your aquarium is not, we must warn, a five-minute job. Indeed, when we hear horror stories of tanks and fishes bought on the same day, we cannot help but wonder how it was done, unless the approach to the job was the same as that to fish-keeping in general – slap-dash!

Your exact plan of action will depend on the type of set-up you have chosen, the type of equipment, and other variables. We will take you through all the steps involved, but you may wish to alter the sequence to suit your own requirements. In any case, we strongly suggest that you make your own personal list of jobs to be done and keep it by you during the actual setting up. As things may get a little damp, it may prove sensible to protect it with a plastic bag or clear film.

Siting the Aquarium

Whatever your set-up and equipment, there are some preliminary considerations and preparations which apply in every case. First, before you even buy your aquarium, you must decide where you are going to put it – not just where it will fit, but the safety and accessibility aspects of its siting. Otherwise it may have a greater impact than intended on your household!

Above: *Periophthalmus* (mudskippers) require a special aquarium with shallow water and exposed rocks or sand onto which they can climb.

Right: The aim is to design your aquarium as a pleasing underwater picture.

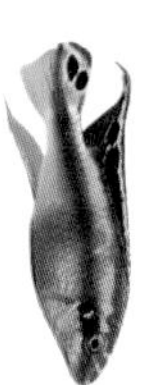

Whatever base you are using for your aquarium must be able to carry the not inconsiderable weight you are planning to put on it. So must the floor beneath! Calculate the volume of your proposed aquarium (internal length x width x height) and use the table of weights and measures at the back of the book to calculate the weight of water involved. This may come as quite a shock – and there is the weight of the tank itself, the stand, and the hood to be considered as well. Equipment supplied specifically for supporting aquaria should have been designed with this consideration in mind; if you are building your own or using a built-in feature in your home, you should seek professional advice from a builder, carpenter, or engineer.

A professionally laid concrete floor should be capable of taking any load you are likely to put on it; the same is not, however, true of wooden floors. These are supported by load-bearing timbers (joists) which run at right-angles to the floorboards and can be located without taking up the floor by looking for the rows of nails where the flooring is nailed down. Heavy loads must be positioned *across* the joists so that the load is spread over several, rather than just one or two. The legs of the stand should be positioned above rather than between joists, as the load will be concentrated at just those four locations. If the stand cannot be positioned as indicated, then stand it on 5 x 10 cm (2 x 4 inch) timbers laid across the joists. You must also consider whether the flooring system can take the planned load at all. If in doubt, on either count, seek professional advice.

One further point, often forgotten until the tank is installed (when it is too late!), is the importance of checking that the proposed site is level – not just side-to-side but also front-to-back. Major irregularities must be compensated for, as otherwise the tank may be unstable; minor ones can be ignored, as long as you don't mind a sloping water surface bearing witness to the actual slope of the floor. Never use small wedges of wood directly under the stand legs as these may split or slip, with disastrous consequences. Instead use pads of exterior-grade plywood of appropriate thicknesses, and at least 10 cm (4 in) square, under the feet of the stand or cabinet. These can also be used to protect floor-coverings from the "stiletto heel effect". Do not use packing pieces if you are using cross-joist supporting timbers; instead plane the latter to size.

Consider whether the proposed location of the aquarium will be safe, for both the aquatic and the other occupants of the household. You do not want to be forever bumping into the aquarium, so there should be no protruding corners near walkways – an alcove is the ideal site. You also do not want accidents to livestock, or broken glass, water, and

Domestic furniture is rarely capable of supporting the weight of any but the smallest aquaria. This chest of drawers is visibly sagging.

fishes all over the carpet, so it should be out of the reach of unsupervized small children and boisterous pets, and of movable furniture such as chairs. If there is no electric wall socket close by, the mains lead must be fixed (with cable clips) to the edge of the floor or the skirting board, never left trailing where it could be tripped over, played with, or chewed. Likewise, make sure no other temptations – such as tins of food, external thermostats and filters, and so on – are left accessible to small fingers, and paws.

On the other hand, the tank should be accessible for viewing and maintenance. Think about the water supply. One of us once maintained 10 aquaria in a bedroom a considerable distance from the kitchen and bathroom taps downstairs, and with the benefit of hindsight, would not do so again! There will also be waste water to be disposed of. Spillages are inevitable when water is carried around – so, given a choice of rooms, perhaps the one with the old carpet would be better.

Preparing for Installation

Think about any help you are going to need when setting up. Unless you are confident about your electrical ability, consider asking a professional electrician to advise on the wiring; you do not want to lose your fishes – or worse, burn the house down – by getting it wrong. Alternatively, seek assistance from an experienced aquarist. Although we do not recommend that beginners do their own electrical wiring, it is important to learn how to from an experienced person, so that you can, for example, wire in a new heater yourself later on.

All but the smallest tanks and stands are best moved by two people, so you will probably need an assistant in the early stages. You may need to organize special transport for a large aquarium, or arrange to have it delivered. Think about the help you *don't* need – arrange for the rest of the family, and pets, to be well out of the way during the proceedings. You will not want any smaller members of the household under your feet, and you may not wish a non-aquatic partner to see what gets spilt on the carpet. Apropos of which, put down plastic sheeting, or at least newspaper, before you start – there is bound to be some mess, so make it easy to clear up, and avoid permanent damage.

As you should have realized by now, there is a lot of planning to be done in advance. Likewise some of the work can be carried out before the actual installation of the aquarium; this will give you more leeway if something doesn't go quite as planned. Make sure you have all the equipment you will require – not just for the aquarium itself, but any necessary tools and accessories. A selection of tools and equipment, including screwdrivers, pliers, scissors, a sharp knife, plugs, cable clips, a spirit level (carpenter's level), insulation tape, and adhesive tape may come in handy. Do not, however, buy your plants in advance; they will not benefit from a period in a bucket somewhere, without proper light and, in the case of tropical plants, probably at the wrong temperature.

Making Decor Items

1 Composite decor items need to be prepared in advance so that the glue has time to dry. Terraces can be made by sticking rocks together. Apply silicon sealant to one rock...

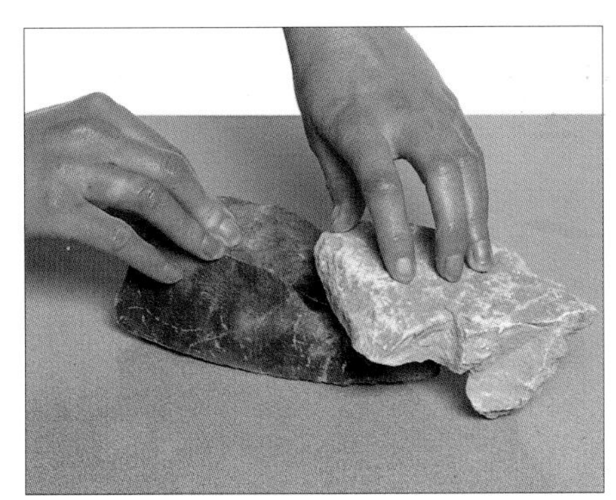

2 ...and press the next firmly into place, securing with tape or rubber bands if necessary. Allow each join to dry before adding further sections.

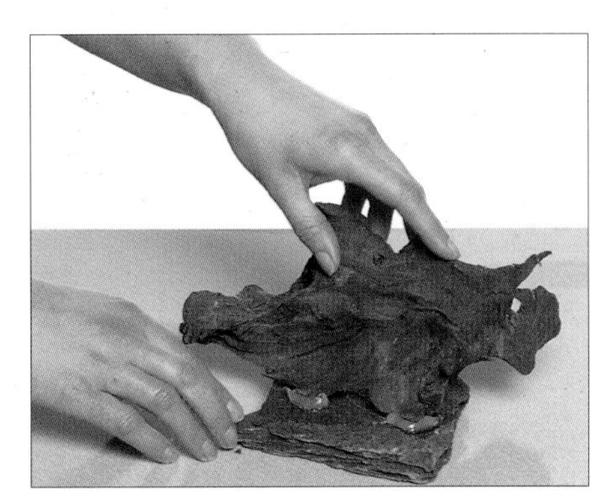

3 Similarly bogwood – and cork bark – can be siliconed to pieces of slate which are subsequently buried in the substrate to prevent the wood from floating away.

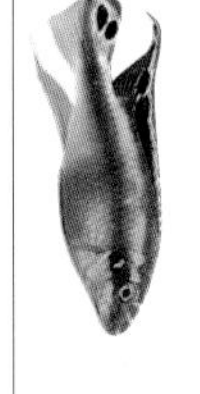

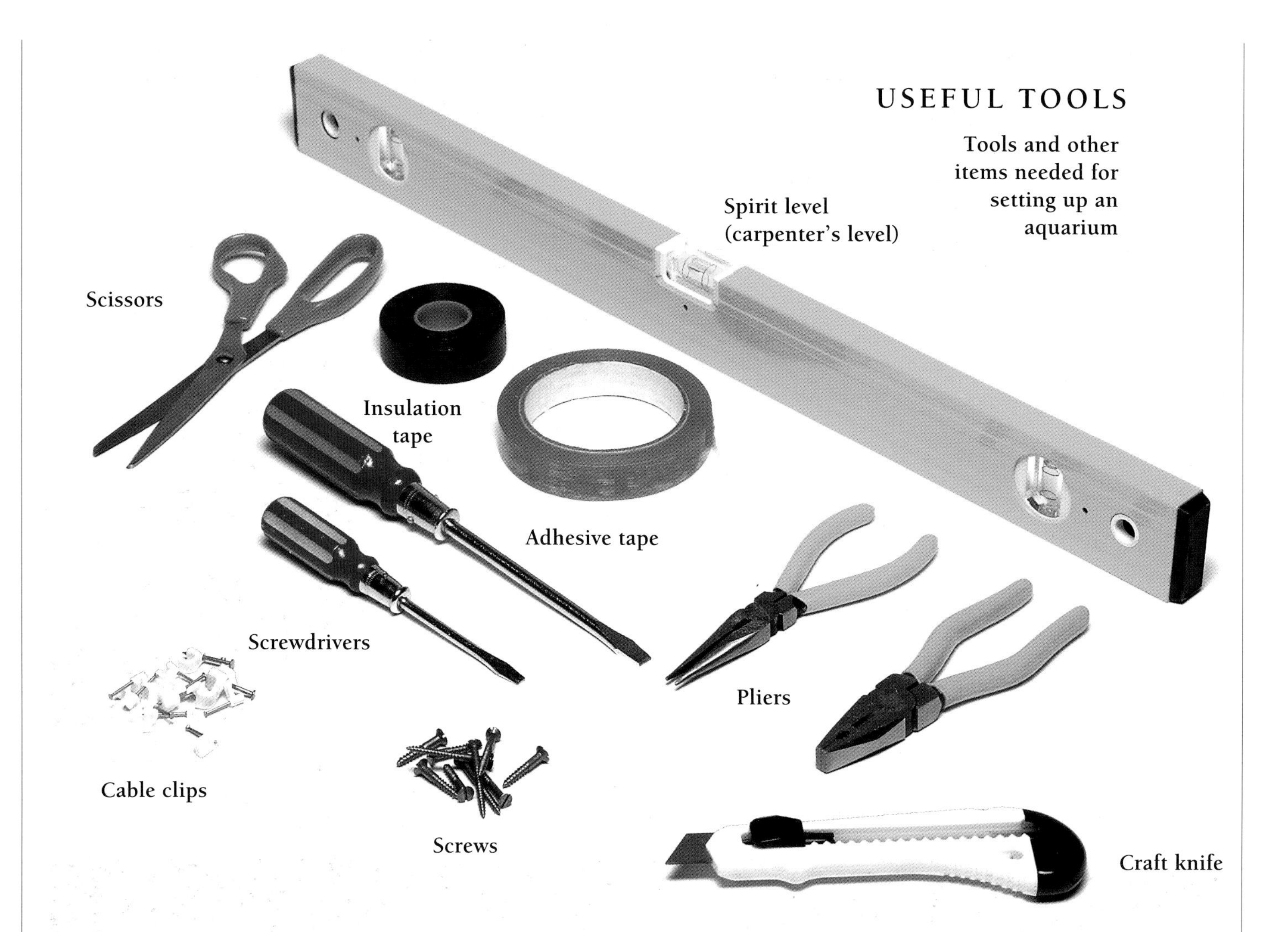

Remember that paints and glues take time to dry. So, if you are painting the back of your aquarium, or sticking something to it to provide a background, you will need to do so at least 24 hours before you can do anything else. (Unless, that is, you are using paper, or "underwater-scene-on-a-roll", which is best applied after the tank is in position, to avoid tearing.) The same applies to siliconing rocks together to form caves or terraces, and varnishing bogwood.

You can wash your gravel (or other substrate) as long as you have somewhere clean to store it afterwards; otherwise you will have to do this rather time-consuming chore on setting-up day, putting each freshly washed batch in the tank as it is ready. Do not skimp on substrate-washing; newly purchased material is often remarkably dirty, and you do not know what that dirt contains – it could be harmful. You must wash your substrate until the water runs clear. This can be done in a plastic

Washing Gravel

Gravel can be washed under the tap in a colander (*left*) or by stirring it vigorously with a spoon in a bucket of water (*right*). The latter method usually involves several changes of water before the gravel is finally clean enough to use, but it is nevertheless normally less wasteful.

colander (bought for the purpose, to avoid detergent residues – and because it will be fit for nothing but gravel-washing after you have finished) under the tap; or by quarter-filling a bucket with gravel and putting it under running water, stirring the gravel with, for example, a wooden spoon. Again the equipment should be specifically for fishkeeping, and not for anything else.

Make sure any other "hard" decor, for example rocks and flowerpots, is scrupulously clean; give everything a good scrub in hot, but *never* soapy, water – soap could leave poisonous residues. Even if you have nowhere clean to store these materials you can get the worst of the job done, and then a quick rinse under the tap will suffice on the day. Take this opportunity to give all rocks a final once-over to make sure there are no suspicious-looking metallic deposits or coloured crystals in them, and discard any you are unsure about.

As previously explained, all-glass aquaria require a baseboard topped with a layer of expanded polystyrene. This too should be prepared in advance. There can be problems persuading the three layers (wood, styrofoam, and glass) to align, and you may wish to avoid problems of this sort by attaching the styrofoam to the baseboard. *Never* use nails or tacks of any kind as these will act as tiny pivots and shatter the bottom glass; instead, use pieces of Blu-tac or double-sided adhesive tape, or a few spots of a suitable glue – that is, one which will not "melt" the polystyrene.

All rocks, flowerpots, bogwood, and other "dirty" items of decor must be scrubbed thoroughly before being positioned in the aquarium. A hard scrubbing or nail brush and plenty of water is all you will need.

Below: **The coldwater aquarium can be just as attractive as its tropical counterpart, and a pleasing backdrop to its occupants, in this case lionhead goldfishes.**

If you are collecting the aquarium yourself it is a good idea to take along the pre-assembled baseboard to protect the bottom of the tank in transit. You should also make sure the tank cannot move around in the car, and protect the glass from knocks and scratching (blankets are useful!). Always lift tanks from beneath, never by the top rails or bracing-bar(s) which are likely to break or come off if subjected to strains of this sort.

Before the tank arrives, however, make sure you have uncluttered access to the house and the "site", and that you have plenty of room in which to work. It will be helpful to have two pieces of timber (say 5 x 5 cm (2 x 2 inches) x tank width) on which to rest the tank (and baseboard) while you install the stand, so that you can easily get your hands underneath to pick it up when the time comes to put it in place. You may wish to add the background at this stage.

Setting Up

When it comes to the actual setting up, obviously the first step is to locate the stand or cabinet (if used) in place. It must be stood squarely on the centre of any supporting pads or timbers; make a final check that it is level (in both directions) using a spirit level (carpenter's level), and that it does not rock (any slight unevenness, however, will be taken out by the load once the tank is filled). Make sure you have left enough space between stand and wall(s) to allow easy access, because you will at some stage need to put your hand into the gap when servicing or replacing equipment.

If you are using a heating mat, then carefully slide the aquarium off the baseboard until you can get your hands underneath to lift it, and put it to one side (on wooden bars, as already described); position the heating mat(s), normally with the cable(s) to the rear, and replace the tank on top.

Preparing and Installing the Tank

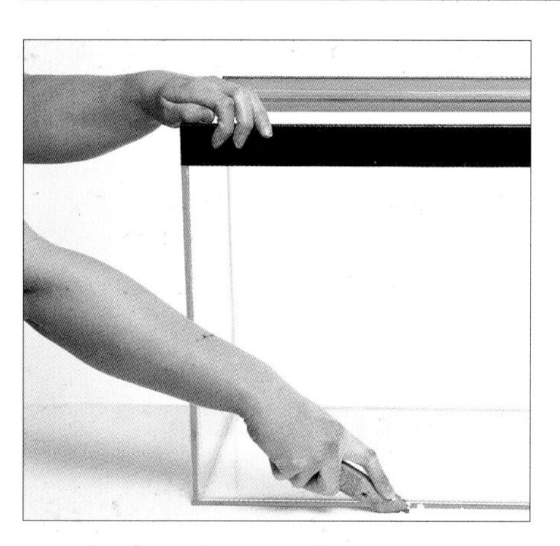

1 Cut a piece of styrofoam the size of the tank base. The easiest method is to use the tank as your template.

2 Place the tank on the styrofoam on the baseboard; you will probably need to have the board cut to size professionally when you buy it.

3 The styrofoam and board can be concealed with tape, or you may prefer a more elaborate method such as a mitred wooden frame for the entire front glass.

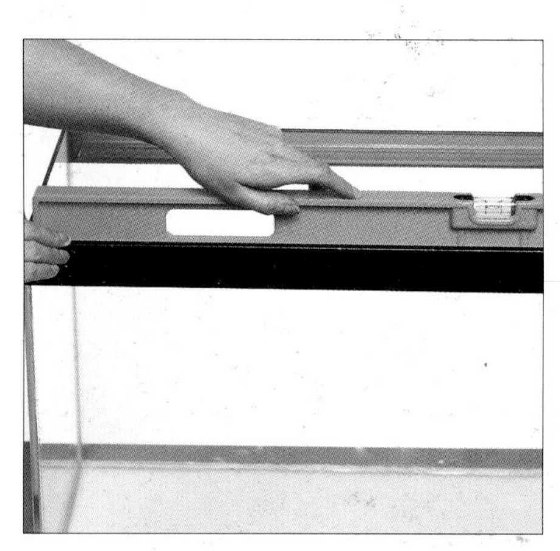

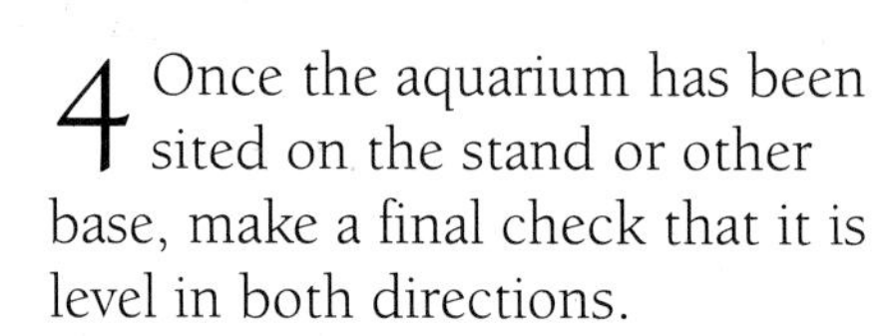

4 Once the aquarium has been sited on the stand or other base, make a final check that it is level in both directions.

5 Internal backgrounds such as cork tiles must be stuck in place well in advance so the glue can dry before the tank is filled. Apply silicon sealant to the glass and press the tiles into place.

Do not be afraid to use plenty of rockwork if designing a Rift Valley cichlid aquarium.

The entire assembly can now be carefully lifted into place on top of the stand (or other base). You should now install your background if you have not already done so.

Next position the undergravel filter plates (if used) *and* uplifts and start adding the washed substrate. If the UG plates don't cover the entire tank floor then hold them down while adding the first few bucketfuls, as otherwise they may slide around and pieces of substrate may get between them and the glass, spoiling the seal.

How much substrate material you add at this stage will depend on your plans for the decor, and whether or not you are using a gravel tidy. You may, for example, wish to bed rockwork down to the bottom of the tank (or the UG plates), and this is sometimes easier, especially with large rocks, if you put in just enough substrate to locate them initially; the rest is added once all your "foundations" and/or terrace supports are in place. You may decide to bend the gravel tidy under these foundations (not easy), or to cut holes in it to accommodate them (but you cannot then alter the decor if you don't like it!). We regard gravel tidies as more of a nuisance than they are worth; excessive digging is better remedied by burying pebbles or small pieces of slate in the substrate as and when (and where) needed. Alternatively, nylon net curtain (bought for the purpose) is much more flexible than standard gravel tidies.

Large heavy aquaria require large solid bases.

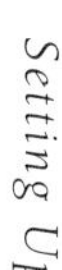

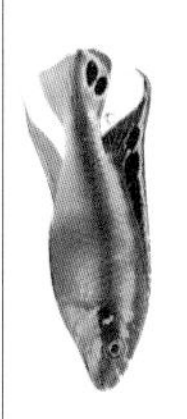

1 Assemble the undergravel filter plate and airlift (if applicable), position in the aquarium, and add a 2.5 cm (1 inch) layer of substrate in which the decor can be bedded.

2 Any rocks – such as this pre-built terrace – should be bedded firmly on the filter plate or tank bottom. Flat-bottomed pieces of rock will be more stable.

3 Add the rest of the substrate material, filling in behind terraces to produce a tiered substrate effect. The surface should be slightly proud of the top of the rocks.

4 Check one more time that the rockwork is stable, and smooth out the surface of the substrate with your hand. The substrate will settle further once water is added.

5 Small light flowerpots do not need to be bedded on the tank bottom (large heavy ones do!), but are simply pushed into the surface of the substrate, making sure the entrance is clear.

6 Flowerpots are not normally found on forest stream beds, so achieve a more realistic effect by hiding them under natural materials. The slate attached to the bogwood (to stop it floating) is carefully worked into the substrate next to the "cave". This bogwood will also help conceal the heater, which will be positioned on the back glass.

7 Complete the hard decor with a piece of artificial wood, which will later be used to conceal the heater cable.

Hard Decor

The installation of the hard decor is one of the most enjoyable parts of setting up, and can equally be one of the most frustrating and irritating experiences, especially if you are using a lot of it. Even if you have drawn up a plan beforehand the materials may refuse to cooperate, or worse, the result may not be quite what you envisaged. Be prepared to fiddle around until you have created a scene you will be happy to live with for some time; the fishes may not appreciate your rearranging their home once they are in it.

Important points to remember are:

1 All rockwork must be securely positioned – rockslides are disastrous and must be avoided at all costs. Foundations of rocky edifices, whether a simple cave or complex pile, should have a reasonably flat underside and be securely bedded right down to the bottom, with plenty of surrounding substrate to retain them laterally. It should be impossible for digging fishes to undermine them; do not, however, worry if substrate is removed along one or two sides, as their weight, the remaining substrate, and any upper layers will keep them in place. Flowerpots are not strong enough to support large heavy rocks, and should be placed in, rather than forming part of the structure of, rocky caves. Ceramic drainpipes, however, are generally made of sterner stuff.

Bogwood and plants make a pleasing backdrop to this *Helostoma temmincki* (kissing gourami).

Heaters and heater/stats are normally held in place by special heater holders, which are attached by suckers to the back or end glasses. They can be installed either before or after the aquarium is filled. Multiple heaters should be evenly distributed to assist even heating. Remember that heat rises, so avoid positioning heater/stats vertically or they may switch off prematurely.

2 Superimposed rockwork should fit securely on to the foundations without rocking. Large pieces will be more secure than small ones, as their weight helps to hold them in place. Never lean superimposed rockwork against the glass, or rely on the glass to keep it in place. Beware of any edifice which could be knocked over – if there is any subsidence it will topple, perhaps injuring fishes, or worse, avalanching through the aquarium glass. These dangers can, of course, be avoided by siliconing rocks together, but if this is done in advance the final effect may not be quite what you had in mind, and if done *in situ* you will need to wait a few hours for the silicon to dry before proceeding further.

3 Until waterlogged (which will take several weeks) bogwood and cork bark will float, and (unless pre-waterlogged by soaking) must be wedged down with rocks. If this is not appropriate they can be anchored to heavy objects with cotton or nylon fishing line; this can be hidden by other decor, and removed later by snipping and pulling. Another method is to silicon a piece of slate to the underside and bury this in the substrate, whose weight will keep the wood in place.

A soft water community of Amazonian fishes.

4 When building terraces remember that substrate material, even with minimum current, will tend to the horizontal and will not take long to flatten out if you slope it. If you want to have different levels you must resort to terracing, using stones to support the upper layers. Even so, material such as gravel will tend to slip between these stones so that you eventually end up with a flat substrate with a wall sticking out of it! It is thus best to design your terraces in advance and silicon the stones of your retaining walls together.

5 Remember to leave spaces for heaters, filters, and other equipment, which will ideally be concealed behind the decor. We do not, however, recommend actually positioning these prior to arranging the hard decor, because of the danger of accidental knocks. Hot water rises, so, even with circulation by means of the filtration, it is best to position heaters just above the substrate to ensure a reasonably even temperature at all levels. Combined heater/thermostats should be positioned horizontally (or at no more than 45° to the horizontal) to avoid the thermostat reacting to rising heat and switching off prematurely. Heaters should not be placed where they may contact (and melt) plastic items, nor too close to plants.

Although you should design your "hardware" so as to accomodate any planting you have in mind, you obviously cannot add the plants until the aquarium has been filled with water, and, for tropical aquaria, warmed up to operating temperature. Plastic plants are, of course, another matter.

Adding Water

You are now ready to add water if you choose; this can then start warming up to room temperature (which will mean less wear and tear on heaters than expecting them to heat the tank from cold) and developing a population of beneficial bacteria. Meanwhile you can be organizing the electrics – perhaps postponing this until the next day if the work so far has taken longer than scheduled. Alternatively you may prefer to install all your equipment before filling the tank – this does have the advantage that there is no risk of getting electrical equipment wet. You do not need to "age" your water – it will be some time before you are ready for the fishes – before filling the tank, but you should treat it, if necessary, to remove nitrates, chloramine, and other pollutants, and soften it if required. You may also need to adjust the pH at this stage.

If you simply tip buckets of water into the aquarium you will disrupt the substrate where the cascade impacts; this can be avoided by placing a plate or bowl (well rinsed to remove every trace of detergent) on the substrate and pouring on to it. Alternatively, if you can manage to pour one-handed, use your spare hand to divert the stream just below the surface.

Place a plate on an open area of substrate, and carefully pour water on to this to avoid disturbing the substrate.

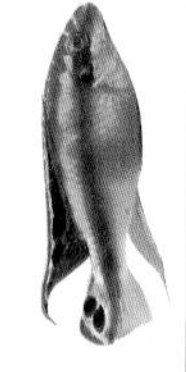

Electrical Wiring

We cannot over-emphasize the need for care when it comes to the electrical wiring, as water and electricity can be a lethal combination – hence the need for professional help. Under no circumstances should you attempt to wire anything yourself – call in a fully-qualified electrician. Once you are up-and-running you should always disconnect the electricity supply before working on the tank as even if the wiring is correct there may still be danger from a cracked heater or other equipment malfunction. In the U.S., make sure to use only "UL approved" devices, and ground all metal surfaces with green wire; especially the fluorescent lamp.

Although it is possible to buy "cable tidies" which wire all the necessary equipment into a single lead to the mains, we prefer not to have all our electrical systems – heating, lighting, and filtration – dependent on a single fuse in the plug at the wall socket. If this fuse blows then everything will go off; fishes might survive a chilling by itself, but chilling plus loss of filtration will be very stressful.

In addition, using a single fuse to protect several electrical circuits is bad practice and potentially dangerous – fuses should *always* be of a suitable rating for the device in question. For these reasons, instead of a cable tidy we recommend a rubber 4-gang multiple socket and individual, correctly fused (protected by circuit breaker), plugs for heating, lighting and filtration circuits. In the U.S. use a multistrip outlet which comes with one circuit breaker that protects the total current. The multiple socket should come ready-fitted with a fuse representing its maximum safe loading, to protect it against overload by the user; the total amperage of devices plugged into the socket must not exceed this rating. The plug connecting the multiple socket to the mains supply should be fitted with a fuse of the same rating. You should also fit a Residual Current Device (RCD) (Ground Fault Interrupter (GFI)) to protect yourself from electrical accident; if you switch off during maintenance, of course, you will be safe anyway, but you should take this extra precaution, to protect your family in case any interference does occur.

The multiple socket (in the U.S. multistrip outlet) approach is also more versatile: cable tidies and multiple sockets can both be screwed on to the outside of the hood (never the inside, as condensation is likely to cause electrical short-circuits), or sited in the cupboard underneath cabinet aquaria. With a multiple socket or multistrip outlet you can also unplug each separate item if it requires attention – for example you can unplug the filter and take it to the sink to clean it, leaving the heaters and lighting running.

A significant number of aquaria suffer terminal disasters as the result of someone unplugging the mains lead; the intention is usually temporary disconnection (for example while vacuuming), but it is all too easy to forget to plug the aquarium back in. A wise precaution against this is to place an explanatory label: "Aquarium – do not touch!" by the mains switch.

Adequate lighting is an important factor in maintaining healthy plants in the aquarium.

Installing Equipment

If you have opted for the multiple socket or multistrip outlet approach the order in which you connect and install your electrical equipment is irrelevant; with a cable tidy, however, things are rather different, because there can be problems moving and repositioning all the equipment once it has been joined together. We suggest the following sequences. Do not attempt to wire the equipment yourself, ask a qualified electrician to do it.

Multiple socket

Wire up equipment and install.
Attach multiple socket or multistrip outlet (with mains lead fitted) to hood.
Fit hood to tank.
Plug in equipment.

Cable tidy

Connect any separate heaters and thermostats.
Install equipment.
Fit cable tidy to hood and wire in mains lead.
Fit hood to tank.
Wire equipment to cable tidy.

The cable tidy/multiple socket should not be plugged into the mains supply at this stage!

Hoods normally come complete with apertures (usually at the back) through which to pass various leads, as it is not a good idea to trap these between the hood and the tank glass – the resulting crimping can damage the cable. One disadvantage of using plugs is that they won't always go through the holes provided – and, of course, if you pass the cable through and then fit the plug, you are left

Xiphophorus (swordtails) are essentially hardwater fishes.

with your equipment irrevocably attached to the hood, just as with a cable tidy. This problem can be solved by cutting slots, of a width to take the cables concerned comfortably, in the bottom rear edge of the hood. If the hood is made of wood the cut surfaces should be sealed with varnish or silicon sealant. Keep the slots as small as possible – large holes may let fishes and water vapour out, and dirt in.

The installation procedure for individual items of equipment is as follows (but always read the manufacturer's instructions carefully as well).

1 Heating

If you have opted for combined heater/thermostats, simply wire the leads into the cable tidy or fit plugs if using a multiple socket (multistrip outlet). If you are using "separates", the heater (or heaters) is connected to the thermostat "power out" cable, while the "power in" cable of the thermostat is wired to the mains (cable tidy or plug). Silicon sealant can be used to good effect to waterproof and insulate the join between heater and "'stat". Even so, make sure the join is never immersed in the tank; ideally pass the cables on either side out through the hood and tape the join to the back of the latter, out of harm's way.

Position internal heaters and thermostats, fixing them in place on the glass with the heater holders which normally accompany them (but can be bought separately). Bi-metallic strip external thermostats are fitted at one end of the aquarium using a specially designed wire clip which fits over the rim. Electronic thermostats are usually attached in a convenient position on the hood, with the sensor fed through one of the wiring apertures into the aquarium. **External thermostats should never be put inside the aquarium**, and due care should be taken to avoid splashing them during tank maintenance.

2 Lighting

The control equipment (choke and starter) for a fluorescent tube is nowadays a single unit with a built-in on/off switch and special leads, with damp-proof (but not waterproof) "cap connectors", to fit the tube. Two clips to hold the tube are usually supplied. The tube itself has to be purchased separately. Start by screwing or bolting the clips to the required positions inside the hood; they should be located 7.5–10 cm (3–4 inches) from the ends of the tube when this is fitted – the next step. Screw the control unit to the outside of the hood, or fit it in the compartment provided (if any) and feed the tube leads through the holes provided (or purpose-cut) in the hood. Fit the cap connectors so that the pins on the ends of the tube are secure in the corresponding slots inside the connector. Wire the controller mains lead to the cable tidy or plug.

Spotlights, whether wall- or ceiling-mounted, come ready-assembled and need only to be screwed to the appropriate surface and connected to the electricity. You may wish to do this by plugging directly into a wall socket, given that the equipment is otherwise completely separate from the aquarium. The descending cable should be clipped to the wall, and, if desired, a wall-mounted on/off switch fitted.

The lighting in this aquarium perfectly displays the iridescent emerald green of the killifish, *Aphyosemion oeseri*.

3 Filters

If the filter is one which has to be filled with one or more media, do this, following the manufacturer's instructions. Air-driven filters (including UG) need simply to be attached to the airpump via the airline (see (4) below). If using an external power filter, run the inlet pipe through the hood, using the suckers provided to fix it in place on the tank side; next hold the outlet pipe below tank level and suck on it until you hear or see water filling the filter chamber. The outlet pipe can then be located in the same way as the inlet; but if you are also using a trickle filter, position the tray(s), attach the spray bar to the power filter outlet, and fix in position above the (top) tray. Internal power filters are normally secured with suckers. Powerheads push-fit on to UG uplift pipes. Run any electrical leads through the hood (for internal equipment), and wire into the cable tidy or to a plug.

A Lake Tanganyika community. Similarly grand rockwork is required for some Lake Malawi cichlids.

Fitting an Airstone to a UG Filter

An airstone can be fitted in the under gravel uplift tube (*above left*) to create a more efficient airlift – but one requiring more air pressure from the pump.

Airlines can be fitted to filters either before or after filling the aquarium, but until the air supply is connected the free end(s) should be secured above water level, or fitted with non-return valves, to prevent accidental siphoning.

An undergravel filter airlift in action (*above*).

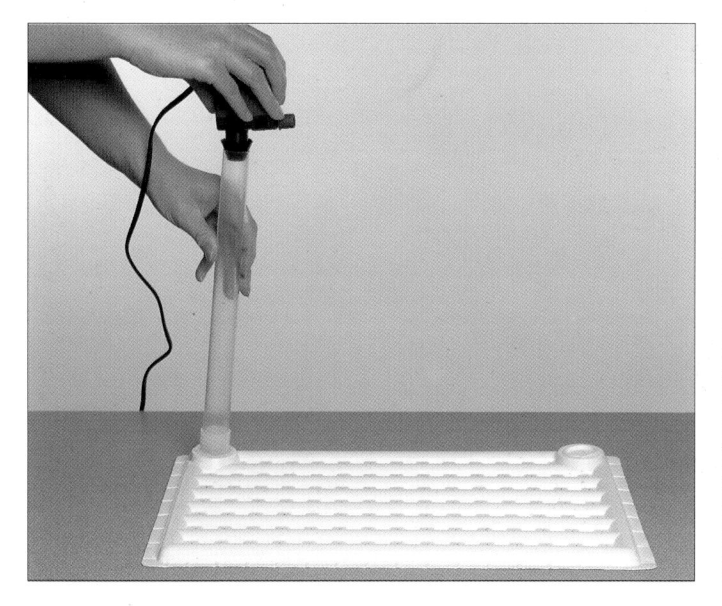

Fitting a Powerhead

Powerheads can be fitted to UG filters already installed in the aquarium, but the top bracing bars of the tank may make this difficult. If this is likely to be a problem the equipment can be assembled beforehand and is then easily manoeuvred into place. Uplift pipes usually need to be shortened to accommodate powerheads, and can easily be cut using a small hacksaw.

Fitting an Internal Power Filter

Internal power filters are normally positioned, using the suckers provided, in one or both of the rear corners, with their outlets directed along the length of the aquarium. To restrict turbulence, however, the outlet can be directed towards the back or end glass.

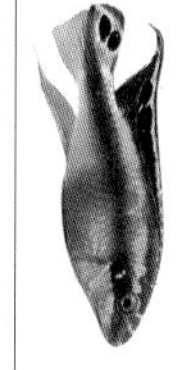

Fitting a Sponge Filter
Sponge filters are best suited to small tanks, and are attached to the rear or end glass using the suckers provided. For optimum effect they should be positioned just above the substrate and angled as shown. The airline is easier to fit before rather than after installation.

Fitting a Box Filter
Box filters are normally located in a rear corner. If installed before the aquarium is filled they are likely to float when water is added; this can be avoided by pre-filling them with some of the water intended for the aquarium: those filled with lightweight media (eg. floss) will benefit from a layer of substrate material above or below the media.

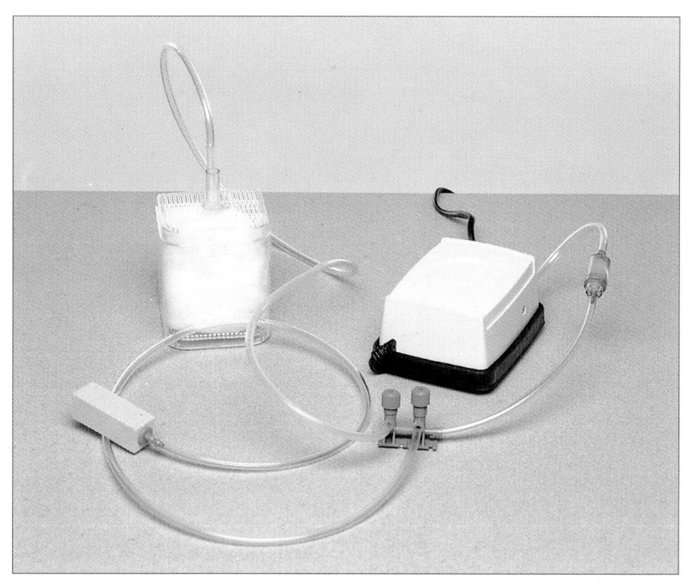

Fitting an External Canister Filter
The inlet and outlet tubes are normally positioned at opposite ends of the aquarium to optimize water circulation and thus debris intake. The inlet – with strainer to exclude gravel, plants, and fishes – is attached to the glass using rubber suckers, with its opening close to the substrate. The outlet can be attached in the same way; or to a spray bar above the water's surface or over a trickle filter; or inserted in an undergravel filter uplift to power reverse-flow UG filtration.

Air Pump
The air pump should be protected from "back-siphoning" by a non-return valve (*right*) sited close to the pump outlet. The air supply can then be split between multiple devices using "gang valves" (*front centre*) which also regulate the amount of air to each device, in this case a wooden diffuser (*front left*) and internal box filter.

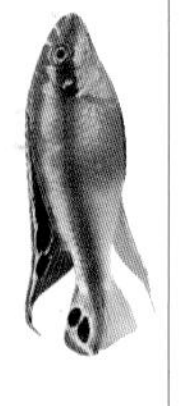

Starting a Filter

1 Powerful filters are sometimes started only after the plants have started to root, to avoid them being displaced by the current. External canister filters are started by the siphon principle, using a siphon starter attached to the outlet (as shown here), or by sucking on the outlet pipe. It is a sensible precaution to do this over a bucket.

2 Once the filter has filled with water, lower the end of the tube (still over the bucket!) below tank level so that the tube fills with water and all air is expelled. A thumb over the end of the pipe will keep air out and water in while the outlet is placed in the aquarium, thus reducing the likelihood of "airlocks" when the power is switched on.

4 Air pump

This should simply be plugged into the electrical supply. Fit any necessary airlines to equipment (for example, UG filters, airstones) and pass out through the holes or slots in the hood. If more than one airline is to be used on a single-outlet pump then the supply must be split using special valves obtainable from your dealer. These fit together to form the size of set required; each set must have an end valve. There is a danger of the individual valves separating in use, and it is a wise precaution to secure them together with insulation tape round the entire set. They can be located inside or outside the hood; the latter usually makes adjustment easier, but this is not necessarily a good thing if you have children.

Air pumps are generally hung from the back of the hood or stood in the cupboard of a cabinet set-up. If an air pump fails for any reason (including powercuts) water may "back-siphon" along the airline, and empty part (or even all) of the aquarium water on to the floor, ruining the pump electrics in the process. Always protect against this by fitting a non-return valve in the airline close to the pump. Alternatively, the pump may be located well above water level, but it has to be said that an air pump on the living room wall is a poor substitute for a Rembrandt!

Having installed all your equipment, store the instructions, guarantees, and shop receipts in a safe place for future reference.

Starting the System

It remains to fix your thermometer in place and, if you have not already done so, to fill the aquarium with water as described above. Connect the mains lead to the electric supply and check that each device is working. Thermostat indicator lights should, with the tank full of cold water, indicate that the 'stat is on; if the heaters are working you should be able to see a slight current of rising water above each, or you can switch off the electricity after they have been on for a few minutes and feel each heater to see if it is warm. If the fluorescent tube fails to light up, try flipping the switch on the control unit!

External power filters sometimes have difficulty dispelling any air trapped inside. Switching off and on again a few times, and/or tipping them gently from side to side, normally does the trick. If not you will need to switch off and suck on the outlet

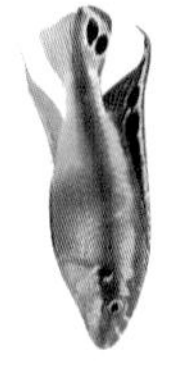

Installing the Thermometer
Internal thermometers (*left*) are best positioned after the aquarium has been filled, to avoid movement and possible damage as the water is added. External liquid crystal display (LCD) thermometers (*right*) can be fitted at any point in the setting up. Take care to get their positioning right, as they will not readily stick a second time, and often cease to function if moved at a later date.

pipe again. Make sure external filters are not leaking, and that trickle filters are emptying properly.

The air supply to the various devices may need adjusting using the valves; if you have a single air-driven item and too much air then, if the pump doesn't have a regulator, fit a double valve in the airline and use the spare to bleed off excess air. This is preferable to the alternative of clamping the airline, which increases back-pressure between clamp and pump and may shorten the life of the pump diaphragm. Over the next few days you may have to tinker with the air supply until it is in perfect balance – it is part of Murphy's Law that air supply initially alters spontaneously without any intervention by the aquarist!

You will probably have to alter the setting on your thermostat(s) at least once before the temperature stabilizes at the desired level. Some 'stats have temperature scales on their adjustment dials, but in our experience these do not always bear much relation to the temperature actually achieved! Expect the 'stat to have a range of 1–1.5°C (2–3°F) between switching on and off; more than that and we would be inclined to take it back to the shop and change it.

Planting

When working temperature has been reached you can buy and add your plants. Once these are installed you should start lighting the aquarium for at least 12 hours each day, and it is a good idea to get into a proper lighting routine so that it becomes habit before the fishes arrive. You should always allow a period of external light (daylight or room light) both before switching the tank light on and after turning it off at night. Sudden changes from "night" to "day" are highly stressful (causing shock), and while "day" to "night" isn't quite so dire, many species will be stressed if forced to spend the night in the open because they had no warning of its approach. If you are likely to be away at "dawn" or "dusk" it is worth having a time switch to operate the tank light and a room lamp on another timer, which is set to come on and go off twice daily at times appropriate to simulate dawn and dusk.

The Maturation Process

You will need to allow about 10–14 days between filling the tank and adding fishes, during which the filtration system will develop the population of bacteria necessary for biological filtration (filter maturation period). At some stage during this period a very high nitrite level will occur; when nitrites have reduced to zero after this peak it will then be safe to begin introducing fishes to the aquarium. It is essential that you ensure the peak has been passed (it might take longer than 14 days) – so monitor nitrite levels every day during this maturation period.

If you fail to take this precaution and add fishes as soon as working temperature has been reached, you will almost certainly experience a phenomenon known by aquarists as "New Tank Syndrome", which is the technical term for the production of fish corpses by means of ammonia and nitrite toxicity. You do not, however, need to monitor ammonia levels as these peak before nitrites, which are thus the critical factor in establishing whether or not the tank is mature.

The bacteria will need something to feed on as they develop, otherwise the minimal numbers present in the water won't increase. There are various ways of achieving this. A small piece of raw meat can be dropped into the aquarium and left to decay, or a pinch of flake can be dropped in daily.

It is now possible to buy special additives which speed up the maturation process - but always monitor nitrite levels rather than relying on time estimates on the container. An alternative solution is to obtain a couple of handfuls of substrate from a mature (and disease-free) tank which can be sprinkled on your substrate to act as a bacterial starter culture.

If you have to clean out your tank at some time in the future, it is worth noting that "used" substrate material, if rinsed clean in cold water, retains a good population of bacteria and tank maturation will be appreciably quicker than it was with new substrate the first time around. Likewise an active filter can be transferred to a new tank, in which case maturation takes very little time at all. Even so, it is always advisable to monitor those nitrites in any newly set-up tank.

Planting

1 Tall plants such as these *Echinodorus* (Amazon swords) are normally sited towards the back of the aquarium, and can be used to help conceal cables and pipes. If possible allow them enough room to spread their leaves in all directions.

2 Small plants can be sited nearer the front, and again used to camouflage unnatural items such as flowerpots. Always check with your dealer that the plant you like is truly aquatic and will flourish under water.

3 It is often more effective to plant groups of a single small species – here *Cryptocoryne beckettii* – close together, instead of a mixture. Do not overplant – in a few month's time what may seem initially sparse should burgeon into an underwater garden.

Finishing touches

1 Once all the decor and equipment is installed fit the condensation tray (or cover glass(es))...

2 ...and finally the hood. It is also advisable to cover the aquarium during any pauses in the setting up, to exclude dust as well as intruders such as insects, pets and children.

3 The water will be slightly cloudy initially; this will normally clear after a day or two, certainly before it has matured sufficiently for fishes to be introduced.

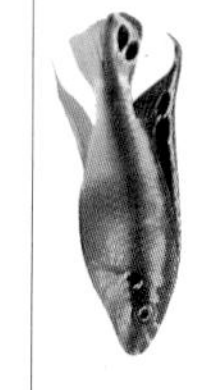

Marine and Brackish-Water Set-Ups

The first thing to consider is the size of your aquarium. It is far easier to maintain a large body of marine water in good condition than a small volume. The minimum recommended size for a marine tank is 100 x 50 x 50 cm (36 x 18 x 18 inches) - if you can accommodate something larger so much the better.

The techniques for setting up marine or brackish water aquaria are exactly the same as for a freshwater tank. The main difference is that you are dealing with water which has had salt added to it and is therefore more corrosive, so you need to avoid using any metallic objects in the aquarium. The breakdown of metals in water can poison your fishes, so extra care is needed when setting up your aquarium.

Ensure that buckets, colanders, spoons, and so on used in preparing water, washing substrate, or whatever, are plastic. If you are using external thermostats, stick them to the aquarium glass – do not hang them over the side of the tank by the wire hanger provided. Likewise heater/thermostat clips –even the clips used to hold fluorescent tubes in the hood – should be non-metallic.

Left: **A mature marine aquarium, with coral fishes, "living rock", and *Caulerpa*, is a stunning spectacle.**

Below: **Although relatively few brackish water fishes are available, they are diverse enough to present an interesting and attractive picture.**

The Water

For the majority of us, the practicalities of collecting our own clean seawater are impossible, as we may live too far from the sea or the seawater may be polluted. Manufacturers can now supply salt to create artificial seawater with the correct balance of minerals for fishes, so that all that needs to be done is to mix the salt with tap water according to the manufacturer's directions until the correct specific gravity is achieved.

1 Calculate the amount of water required – as the decor occupies part of the aquarium volume, and accuracy is essential, the easiest way is to fill the aquarium using a bucket of known volume which is then multiplied by the number of bucketfuls. Put the required amount of salt (in accordance with the manufacturer's instructions) in a plastic bucket.

2 Mix the salt with water so that it is at least partially dissolved before adding to the aquarium. During partial water changes – as opposed to initial filling – the salt should be completely dissolved so that the correct aquarium salinity is achieved virtually immediately.

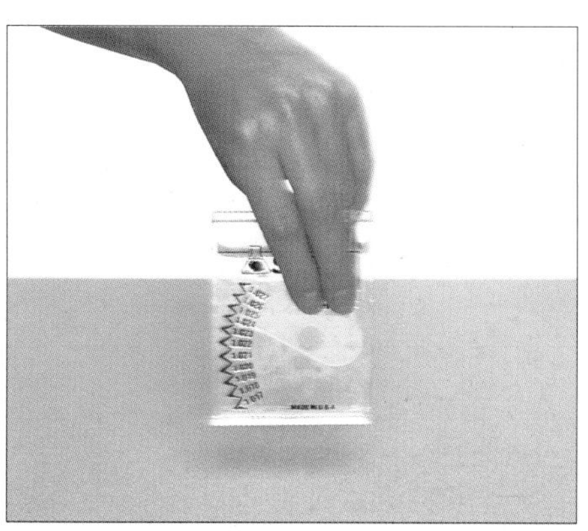

3 Check the aquarium salinity with a hydrometer after initial filling and then after every partial water change and evaporation top-up.

Specific gravity (SG) is measured using a hydrometer and is a scale showing the total amount of dissolved salts in the water. This can also be measured in grams per litre but in the hobby is usually expressed in terms of SG. The SG varies with the water temperature, for example, a salinity of 17.2 gm per litre gives an SG reading of 1.020 at 15°C (50°F) and 1.017 at 25°C (77°F). The range we require for marines is 1.021 to 1.024 at a temperature of between 24° and 25°C (75° and 77°F).

For brackish-water fishes the SG can vary considerably as these fishes may be found in anything from virtually fresh to almost totally marine waters. Most are estuarine species, so the salinity they experience can vary from hour to hour as the tide comes in and goes out. In the aquarium, it has been found that mixing salt to half the strength recommended for marines works very well for brackish-water species.

When evaporation occurs, it is pure water that is lost; the salts remain in the aquarium, so do not top up the aquarium with more salt water or you will increase the SG. At times of high evaporation, that is midsummer, top up the aquarium with fresh water. If you are carrying out a partial water change and refilling with fresh salt water, ensure that you check the SG. A well-fitting cover glass will reduce the amount of water lost through evaporation.

It is very important to check the nitrite and ammonia levels during the maturation period and ensure that your filtration system is beginning to function efficiently. The length of the maturation period will vary from aquarium to aquarium and there is no really successful way of speeding it up to any great degree, so just be patient and let nature take its course – slow and steady is far better than fast and dangerous! The use of a protein skimmer in the system is beneficial as this helps to reduce the amount of toxic waste at an early stage; indeed, many marine aquarists would not consider a set-up complete without a protein skimmer.

Lighting

The amount of lighting required depends on what you intend to keep in the marine aquarium. For the purposes of this book, we will be dealing only with fishes, so the amount of light required is simply what is sufficient to see them by. If you are considering marine invertebrates the lighting becomes a whole new ball game and you will need to do your homework in other, more specialized publications. For the majority of aquaria, a combination of two fluorescent tubes will be adequate, say a daylight and an actinic blue. "Gro-lux" may enhance the colour of the fishes, but red light is absorbed first by seawater so it will not illuminate your aquarium as well as the actinic blue, which will penetrate the water furthest.

Decor for Marine Aquaria

The best substrate for a marine aquarium is coral sand. However, this is expensive and many people like to use a coarser substrate of crushed tufa as a base and overlay it with coral sand. In order to avoid the sand disappearing between the larger pieces of rock, place a gravel tidy over the first layer of substrate before adding the coral sand.

Tufa rock can form the basis of your "reef". It is a very crumbly rock and cannot be glued together, so be sure to seat the pieces well. Fishes dig, and if they undermine your structure this can have dire results such as cracked tanks, flooded living rooms, and a great deal of explaining to be done to the non-fishy members of the household! So seat the rocks securely on the bottom, and build carefully

Below: **"Living rock" may include a fascinating variety of organisms such as this tubeworm, but also unwelcome invaders such as small crabs. Marine invertebrates are even more delicate than coral fishes.**

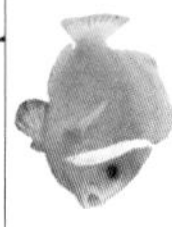

The variety of form and colour of coral fishes is almost endless. Here we see *Centropyge loriculus* (flame dwarf angel) (*bottom*), with corals, fan-worms, and *Labroides dimidiatus* (cleaner wrasse) (*top*).

using large pieces that interlock well rather than a lot of smaller, easily dislodged pieces.

An alternative to tufa rock is lava rock, which is darker in colour and of a different texture. Depending on the type of fishes you are keeping, you may also like to add clusters of giant barnacle shells to provide hiding places for smaller species. If you use other shells, ensure that the fishes cannot become trapped in them. Dead corals are available but the ethics of using them is down to the individual. Some have been obtained by destroying a reef, killing the coral and bleaching it clean for use in the aquarium, while others are collected by hand so that only prime specimens are used. A far more environmentally friendly substitute is artificial coral. Once this has a growth of algae on it, it blends in quite nicely.

Whatever final design you use, ensure that there is a free flow of water around the aquarium. The rocks will be hiding the heater/thermostat but you still need to be able to get at this should it fail without having to demolish the decor. It is also essential that water flows over the heater so that it does not overheat and burn out.

Your "reef" can be enhanced by the addition of some pieces of "living rock" but make sure that you have high enough lighting levels to maintain it. Living rock is now being cultured artificially in an effort to conserve natural reefs.

Decor for Brackish Aquaria

Rocks, plants and wood may be employed as decor for the brackish-water aquarium, but check that the plants are salt-tolerant before using them. Brackish-water aquaria normally have the appearance of a freshwater biotope, with all the possible variations that may entail; the main difference between fresh- and brackish-water aquaria is that the water has salt added and it is therefore necessary to take care to avoid metal fittings in the system.

1 The background should be appropriate to the planned occupants; coral reef "background on a roll" is available.

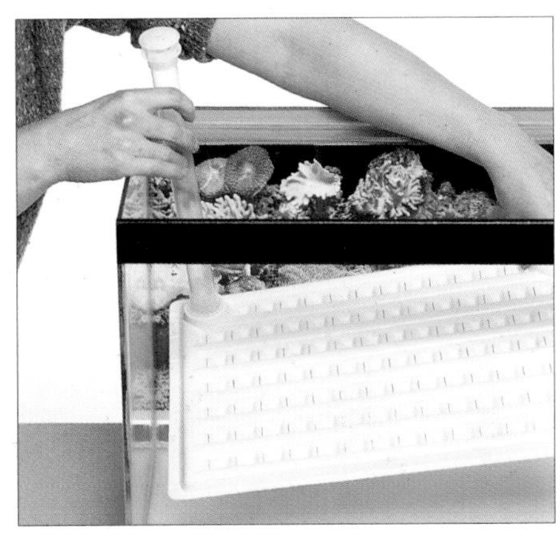

2 Install the undergravel filter plate(s) and uplift(s) if this type of filtration has been chosen.

3 Add a thin layer of substrate material (coral sand is used in this set-up).

4 Bed the foundation rocks (tufa is used here) firmly into the substrate so they rest on the filter plate (or bottom of the tank). Use large stable pieces of rock to create a solid basis for the imitation reef.

5 Add the remainder of the substrate, filling in between the foundation rocks. Roughly level the surface of the substrate by smoothing it out with your hand.

6 Build up the "reef", ensuring each piece of rock seats securely on the layer beneath. The importance of stable rockwork cannot be over-emphasized even when working with tufa.

7 Add corals and any other decorative items, again ensuring these are securely positioned.

8 The finished decor. Once algae have grown on the rocks and corals the "reef" will look far more natural than it does at this stage.

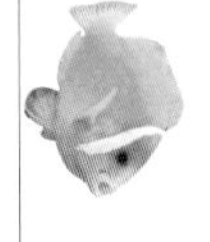

Buying and Adding the Fishes

While your tank matures put the final touches to your shopping list of fishes, perhaps visiting local shops to check what is available – and resisting any temptation to buy! You can, if you wish, reserve fishes, but expect to have to leave a deposit or even pay in full. It is, however, worth reserving only unusual species not generally available; remember too that come "the day" you may be left with the poorer-quality specimens no one else wanted.

You should already have calculated the number of fishes your aquarium can accommodate; you must now decide whether to introduce them all at once, or in stages (remember the filter will have to adjust to the increased loading). If you intend buying juveniles you will be imposing only a fraction of the planned eventual load, and can add them all at once. It may, however, be sensible to introduce adults in two or three batches with a few days between. It is usual to introduce marines a single fish at a time.

Before we discuss buying and introducing fishes, a few words on stress. Being caught, bagged, transported, and released into a strange environment is a highly stressful experience for a fish.

Above: Puffer fishes are found in fresh, brackish, and sea water so make sure you get the right type for your aquarium. This is *Tetraodon palembangensis*, a freshwater species.

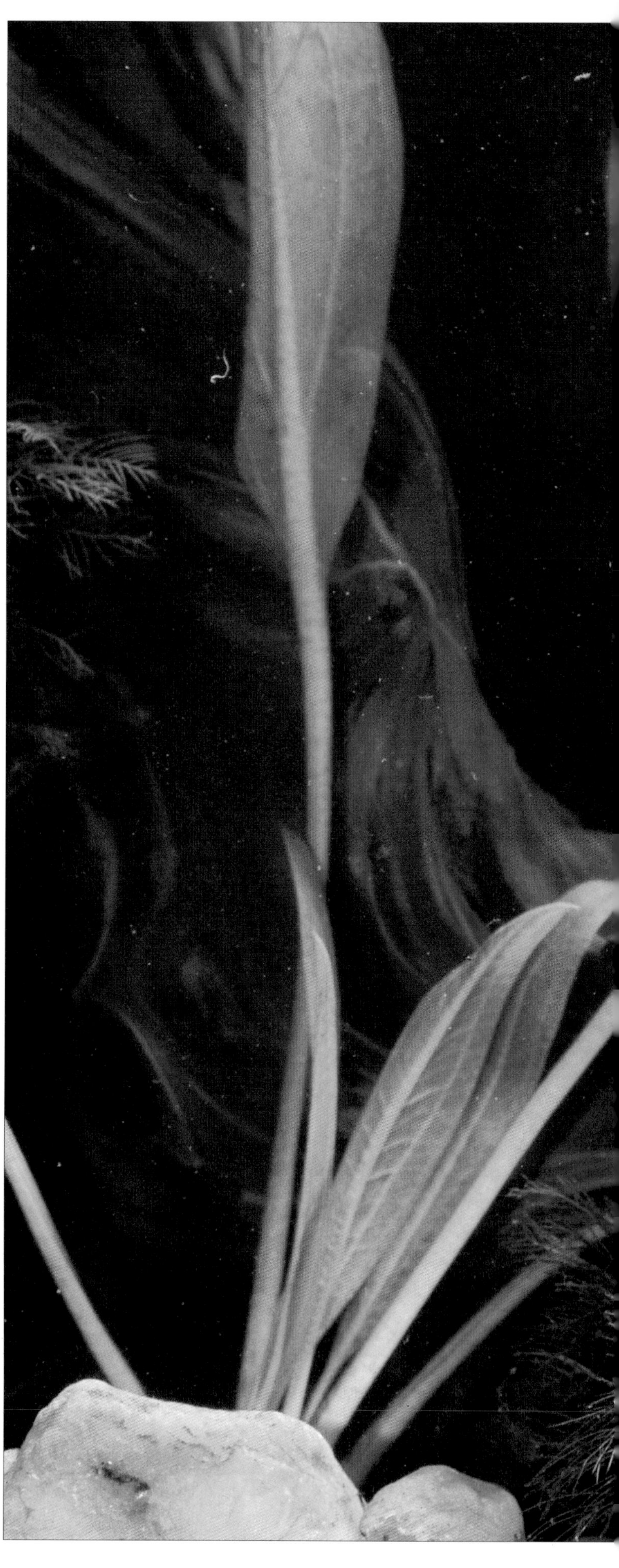

Right: Poecilia species (sailfin molly). The raised dorsal fin of the displaying male has been damaged and regenerated at the front. This fish would never win prizes, but will not pass on its defect to its offspring.

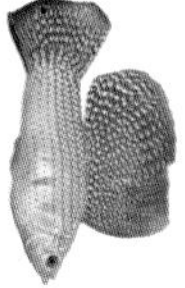

When buying a fish, ask the dealer to trap it between net and front glass, then make a final check that it is a good quality, healthy specimen. This is a standard procedure so do not be afraid to insist.

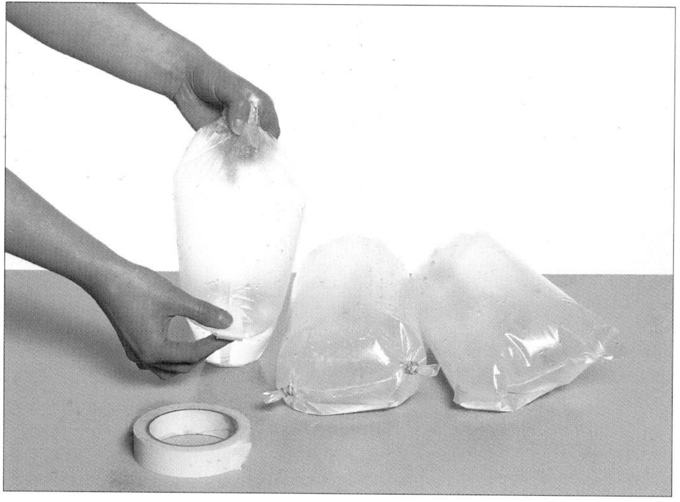

Bags should be "cornered" for small fishes, to prevent them being trapped and injured. Right to left: bag with welded corners, corners tied with rubber bands, corner being taped "square".

Stress can kill, so minimize the upset. Avoid buying fishes which have just arrived at the retailer's as they need time to recover from that last upheaval.

Pick a quiet time for your shopping, when the dealer can give you his or her undivided attention. When buying fishes you are perfectly entitled to choose specific individuals, although in practice if there is little difference between most of a particular batch it is more appropriate to reject instead of select, simply refusing any which are deformed or undersized. Ask the dealer to hold each fish in the net against the tank front while you give it a final once-over. Never buy from a tank containing diseased or dead fishes – the rest may be dead in a few days. Be particularly selective if buying breeding stock: you want only the best, as poor quality parents usually produce poor quality fry which you won't be able to sell.

The dealer will pack your fishes in polythene bags, usually putting these in brown paper bags or a carrier so the fishes won't be frightened by what is going on around them. Fishes more than 7.5 cm (3 inches) long, and adults of territorial species (for example cichlids), should always be bagged singly to avoid murders in transit. If the dealer won't comply, shop elsewhere! Ideally take along suitably sized lidded buckets for very large specimens.

If you will be travelling some distance ask the dealer to "double-bag" (in case of leaks) and to fill the air space in the bags with oxygen. For long journeys, or in very hot or cold weather, take along an insulated container – a "cool box", a cardboard box lined with styrofoam, or a proper fish box borrowed from a friend. If you are buying a lot of

Left: **Fishes should be transported in darkness to keep them inactive and to avoid stress. Brown paper bags are commonly used for this purpose.**

Below: **An insulated container – this is a styrofoam "fish box" – is useful for maintaining the correct temperature during transportation.**

Paracheirodon innesi (neons) should be kept in a shoal – but don't expect them to all face the same way.

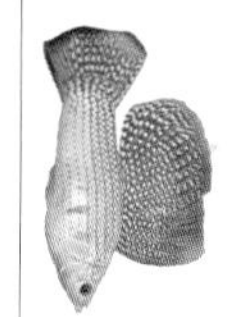

fishes most dealers will supply a box if asked. Head for home straight away, and resist the temptation to keep checking the fishes in transit – every time you let light in you will be causing stress.

On arriving home, remembering the need to avoid undue stress, keep handling to a minimum: take out each bag in turn, undo it, and float it in the tank to let the temperatures equalize. Secure the top by trapping it with the hood or clipping it to the tank edge with a clothes peg, otherwise it may sink and release the fishes prematurely. Repeat this process for the other bags. Equalization normally takes only minutes; check with a thermometer, and once the temperatures are within a degree or so of each other the fishes can be released. The longer a fish is floated, exposed and with nowhere to hide, the greater the stress, especially when the tank is already occupied by inquisitive fishes. Submerge the top of the bag, ensure it is wide open, then gently tip the fishes out. Always check they are all free!

Although you will be eager to watch your new pets, they will be frightened and confused, so turn the tank light off; the room light (or daylight) will suffice for them to settle in. Next morning turn the room light on about 30 minutes before the tank light, and make this part of your normal routine. Never the other way round; sudden changes from "night" to "day" (and *vice versa*) are extremely stressful. Resist the temptation to feed your fishes for the first 24 hours; let them recover from their upheaval, then feed lightly, gradually increasing daily rations to maximum, so that the filter can take up the additional loading.

Subsequent Additions

If, after a few months, you want to add another fish or two (only if this doesn't mean overcrowding), you won't want to risk introducing disease, so it is worth investing in a quarantine tank. This must be large enough for its temporary inmate(s) and set up and matured as for a permanent aquarium, except that decor can be rudimentary, just enough to provide shelter. The water chemistry should be what the newcomer has been used to; adjust it (if necessary) to match your aquarium during the quarantine period (normally two to three weeks). This period will also allow the new fish(es) to recover from transit and adapt to your routine before meeting future tankmates.

Introducing New Fishes to the Aquarium

1 Undo the bag and float it in the aquarium to let the temperatures equalize. Secure the bag (for example with a clothes peg) so that it cannot sink and release the fishes prematurely.

2 When the temperatures are approximately equal (within a degree), submerge the neck of the bag, holding it wide open with one hand, and gently tip the fishes out.

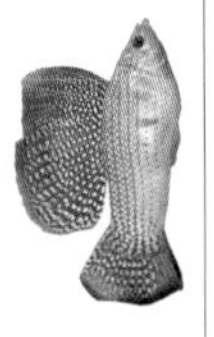

Above: This quarantine tank contains just the basics for the physical and psychological well-being of its occupant(s): heater/'stat and (UG) filter, and decor which provides shelter but leaves the fish(es) visible for observation.

Always check nitrate levels (and remedy if necessary) before introducing new fishes to an established aquarium; your fishes will have adjusted gradually to any slow increase in nitrate, but a newcomer may suffer toxic shock if suddenly exposed to a high level. Many mystery deaths in new fishes are probably due to this.

Finally, sooner or later you will visit a retailer's and fall for a fish about which you know nothing. The temptation to buy it will be overwhelming, but you must resist – our golden rule about doing your homework first never ceases to apply!

Below: Some fishes are attractive and charming as small juveniles, and are often mistakenly purchased for community aquaria. Unless you do your homework you may end up with a "monster" like this *Astronotus ocellatus* (oscar).

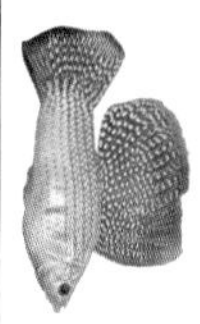

Keeping them Healthy

General Maintenance

Maintenance is largely a matter of continuing to apply the principles learned when setting up your aquarium, thus ensuring continued optimal living conditions for your fishes. What is needed, and how often, depends on the individual aquarium and its occupants, and must be determined by you, the aquarist; the routine suggested below is suitable for the average general community.

Daily: Check temperature, health of fishes, and that equipment is working.

Weekly: Make a 25 per cent water change, siphoning any accumulated debris from the substrate surface. Remove dead vegetation. Check nitrite level.

Monthly: Clean filter(s); "hoover" gravel if necessary. Check nitrate level.

Remember to adjust the chemistry and temperature of "new" water to match tank conditions, and to eliminate any nasties such as chlorine. Filter and substrate maintenance disrupts bacterial populations, so reduce feeding for a couple of days before and after monthly maintenance sessions.

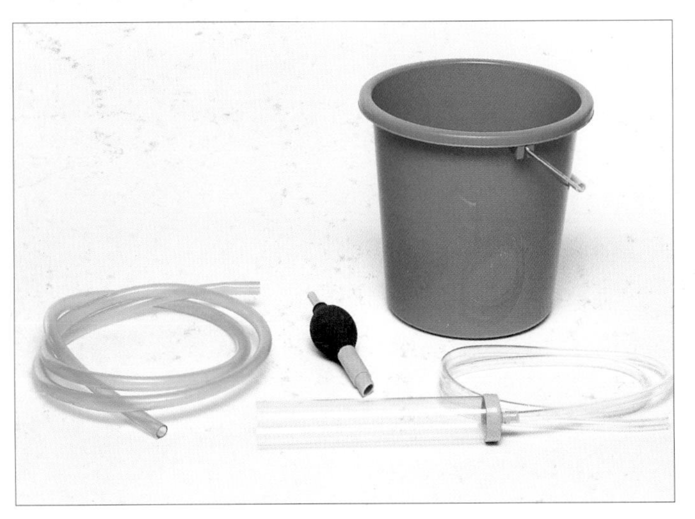

For routine maintenance you will need a bucket and a piece of tubing for siphoning off water from the aquarium. Optional extras are a gravel cleaner (*bottom right*) and siphon starter (*centre*), though many aquarists start their siphon simply by sucking the tube.

Right: Bottom-sifting _Corydoras_ catfishes may suffer damage to their delicate barbels if kept over a coarse substrate.

Siphon off the required amount of water, using the siphon to remove any "mulm" (accumulated debris) and other detritus. Take care not to siphon off fishes or plants! If the tank is sited near a window or outside door, it is quicker, with less risk of spillages, to siphon on to the garden using a long tube, instead of into a bucket.

The substrate can be "hoovered" periodically with a gravel cleaner, taking care not to uproot plants. Avoid excessive hoovering, however, especially where undergravel filtration is used, as it disrupts populations of beneficial bacteria living on and in the substrate.

When refilling, pour the new water into the palm of your hand to avoid disturbing the substrate and decor. Alternatively stand the bucket on the hood and siphon the new water into the tank.

Obviously, action is required if any check reveals a problem. Counter high nitrite with twice-daily 25 per cent water changes until the level returns to zero; identify and eliminate the cause(s) – for example over-feeding or inadequate or interrupted filtration. An increase in nitrates suggests a need for larger (maximum 30 per cent) or more frequent water changes, or adjustments to the tank population or feeding regime.

The importance of regular observation of the fishes cannot be over-emphasized; abnormal behaviour – loss of appetite, clamped fins, increased respiration, scratching or shimmying – is usually the first warning of an environmental problem or outbreak of disease. Prompt action may make all the difference.

Diagnosis and Treatment of Illness

There are three main points to remember about illness in the aquarium:

1 At least 95 per cent of illnesses are environmental rather than pathogenic (caused by an outside organism). Moreover many pathogenic diseases remain dormant unless the fish is weakened by environmental factors.
2 There is no point in medicating a fish unless you know exactly what is wrong.
3 Prevention is better than cure.

Point 1 is a bitter pill to swallow when you have tried to provide optimal conditions; many aquarists find it impossible to accept, and continue to kill their fishes while laying the blame elsewhere. A small closed ecosystem is, however, extremely vulnerable to imbalance or overload, even in experienced hands, so always suspect environmental causes (unless pathogenic disease is obvious); even if water quality checks out OK an extra water change does no harm, and often effects a cure.

Point 2 may sound obvious, but many aquarists panic when a fish falls ill, administering a succession of patent remedies in the hope of hitting the right one. The resulting chemical brew is more likely to poison the entire aquarium. Remember that fishes, like us, suffer organ failure, so a single corpse is a reason for concern, but not alarm. If more fishes become ill, and you cannot identify the cause, seek help from other more experienced aquarists or your vet, who should be able to arrange post-mortem diagnosis. Few vets routinely offer this service, so discuss the possibility before the need arises.

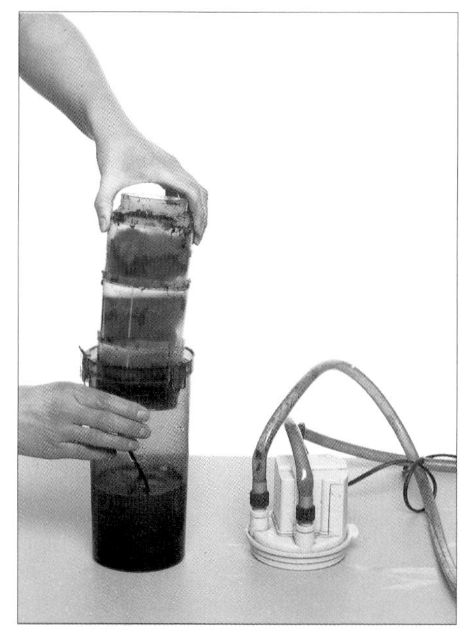

1 Unplug the filter from the mains, carefully remove it from the tank, and take off its top. Lift out the dirty media. This can be a messy job, and is best performed over the sink or bath – or outdoors if weather permits.

2 Remove the media from any refillable internal containers. Part (no more than 50%) of the used media can be discarded if desired. The remainder should be re-used to maintain continuity of bacterial action.

3 Rinse the remaining media (in this instance, filter floss) in a bucket of tank-temperature water (ideally tank water) to remove the worst of the dirt. Thoroughly rinse out the filter canister and any internal containers.

4 Refill the internal containers with recycled and replacement media.

5 Replace the containers in the filter canister.

6 Replace the top and secure. The filter is now ready to be re-installed in the aquarium.

Once a specific disease is diagnosed you can normally obtain the appropriate medication from a dealer, or, in the case of prescription drugs, the vet. Always follow any instructions to the letter, not only using the correct dosage, but completing the full course of treatment; otherwise you may destroy active pathogens, but not those waiting to hatch. Avoid medicating healthy fishes by treating non-infectious patients in a hospital tank (your quarantine tank in another guise) or by "spot treatment" (for example for fungus), after which the fish is returned to the community.

Remember that some medications – for example copper-based treatments – are toxic to some fishes. Some may harm plants, marine invertebrates, and beneficial bacteria in your filter, and should, where possible, be used only in the hospital tank.

Prevention (point **3**) includes correct setting-up, suitable maintenance, quarantine of all new arrivals, and constant observation of your fishes. But beware of "transferred hypochondria", a serious malady which affects all aquarists at some stage, leading them to imagine their fishes are suffering every ailment in the book. Not wishing to encourage this, we will cover only a few of the commonest problems here:

Symphysodon **species (discus) are particularly prone to Hexamitiasis (hole-in-head disease).**

Constipation

Symptoms: reduced appetite; minimal or no faeces; the fish may have a slightly swollen abdomen and/or rest on the bottom of the tank.
Cause: incorrect diet or over-feeding.
Treatment: half a level teaspoon of magnesium sulphate (Epsom salts) per 4.5 litres (1 gallon) . If the fish recovers, improve the diet.

Dropsy/"Malawi Bloat"

Symptoms: swollen body, especially the abdomen, due to build-up of fluid in the tissues.
Cause: environmental, or organ failure. "Malawi bloat", which affects East African mouthbrooding cichlids, is caused by excessive salt (sodium chloride) levels, high nitrates, or unsuitable diet.
Treatment: none; remedying the cause occasionally effects a cure.

Fin-rot

Symptoms: fin membranes disintegrate and the rays become inflamed.
Cause: bacterial, triggered by poor water quality or injury to the fins.
Treatment: remedy the cause; spot treatment with gentian violet.

Fungus

Symptoms: white fluffy growths on body/fins.
Cause: fungus attacks areas where the protective mucus coating is damaged by injury, parasites, or environment.
Treatment: remedy the cause; spot treatment with gentian violet, or use an aquarium fungicide for major outbreaks.

Gill Parasites

Symptoms: scratching, laboured respiration (both, however, normally symptoms of environmental problems); in severe infestations heightened colour, glazed eyes, and loss of motor control as oxygen shortage affects the brain.
Cause: usually flukes (*Dactylogyrus*).
Treatment: "Sterazin", from aquatic dealers.

Hole-in-Head

Symptoms: white stringy faeces; sometimes enlarged, pus-filled sensory pores on the head. Affects mainly cichlids.
Cause: *Hexamita*, an internal parasite normally harmful only when the fish is weakened by other factors (age, stress, environment).

This *Colisa sota* (honey gourami), seen here in a "hospital tank", is distended through dropsy.

A *Xiphophorus* species (platy) with a patch of fungus on its head, probably following an injury.

This *Microgeophagus altispinosa* is suffering from Hexamitiasis (hole-in-head disease).

A *Gasterosteus aculeatus* (3-spined stickleback), its belly distended with a tapeworm. Internal parasite infestations are not usually so obvious.

Exophthalmus (pop-eye) is usually triggered by poor water quality.

Treatment: metronidazole ("Flagyl") or di-metronidazole (prescription drugs); 50 mg per 4.5 litres (1 gallon) mixed with water before use; repeat after three days.

Intestinal Parasites

Symptoms: emaciation despite good appetite; worms sometimes protrude from the vent.
Cause: various species of intestinal worms.
Treatment: a suitable anthelminthic (from the vet) administered in food.

Large Skin Parasites

Symptoms: scratching; individual parasites are visible on skin.
Cause: fish lice (*Argulus*) are round and almost transparent, lying flat against the skin; anchor worms (*Lernaea*) are worm-like, attached at one end; leeches are also roughly worm-like but attached at both ends. All are more common in ponds than in aquaria.
Treatment: remove with tweezers, and apply antiseptic to the site. For serious pond infestations treat with 1.125 – 1.8 mg per 4.5 litre (1 gallon) of Metriphonate (an insecticide).

Life Cycle of the Fish Louse

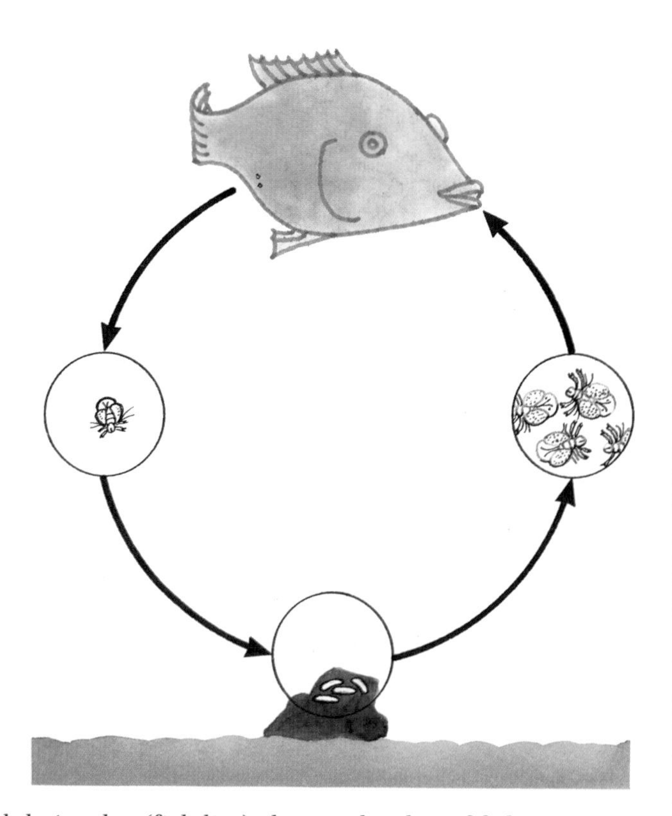

Adult Argulus (fish lice) cling to the skin of fishes. Mature females leave the host and lay their egg capsules on any hard surface; the young hatch after 4 or more weeks. When mature they seek out a host fish. Treatment of the water is effective against adults and juveniles.

Fin damage (for example, after battles between cichlids) often leads to infection with bacterial fin-rot. Severe cases can result in death or permanent deformity.

Pop-Eye (Exophthalmus)

Symptoms: the eye protrudes from its socket, which is inflamed.
Cause: usually environmental, rarely parasitic (which is incurable).
Treatment: correct water quality/chemistry. Recovery may take several days.

Skin Slime Disease

Symptoms: scratching/shimmying; a fine grey coating on body/fins.
Cause: parasites of the genera *Costia, Cyclochaeta*, and/or *Chilodonella*; these generally attack only when the body mucus has been affected by poor environment.
Treatment: use a proprietary remedy; correct water quality/chemistry.

Swim Bladder Disease

Symptoms: loss of balance, swimming upside-down or on on side.
Cause: a) swim bladder bruised during handling, fighting, or breeding; b) bacterial infection, usually associated with poor water quality.

Life Cycle of the Anchor Worm

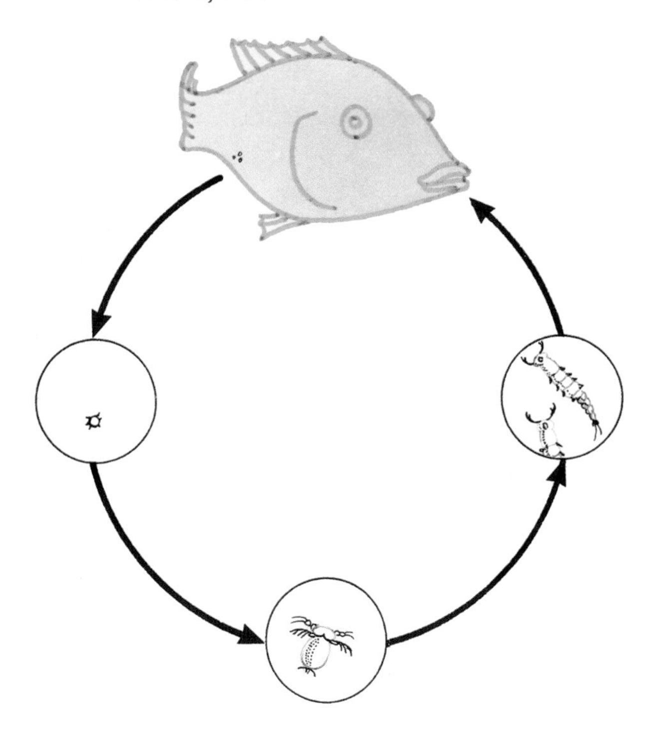

Females anchored to the host's skin release eggs into the water. Juveniles seek out a host and moult before attaining maturity. Males die after mating, leaving the females to renew the cycle. Adults can be removed manually from the host, while juveniles can be elimated by treatment of the water.

Life Cycle of the Fish Leech

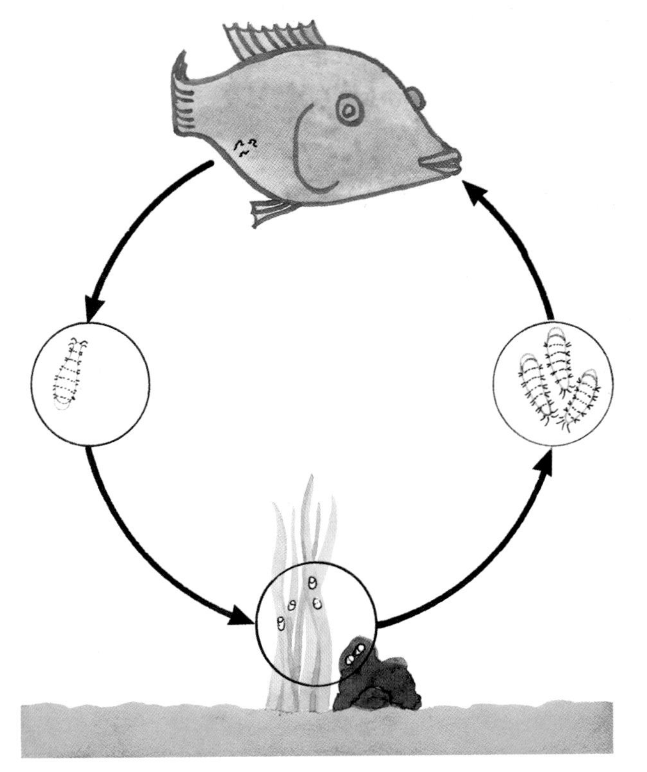

Adult leeches suck their hosts' blood, but detach themselves to lay eggs in oval cocoons on rocks/plants. The young leeches need to find a suitable host to survive. Control is by removal of adult leeches from the fish, and of decor which may harbour eggs.

Treatment: transfer fish to shallow water; for b) improve water quality and treat the fish with a broad-spectrum antibiotic. If there is no improvement after a week, consider euthanasia.

Velvet
Symptoms: a golden velvety coat on body/fins; scratching, increased respiration.
Cause: the parasite *Oodinium*.
Treatment: use a proprietary remedy.

White Spot
Symptoms: tiny white spots on body/fins; initially few, increasing dramatically after a few days.
Cause: the parasite *Ichthyopthirius*.
Treatment: use a proprietary remedy.

Finally, we suggest you do not keep a medicine chest. Buy medicines only when you need them, as you will then be less likely to panic dose unnecessarily or incorrectly.

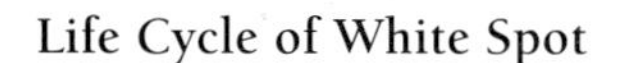
Life Cycle of White Spot

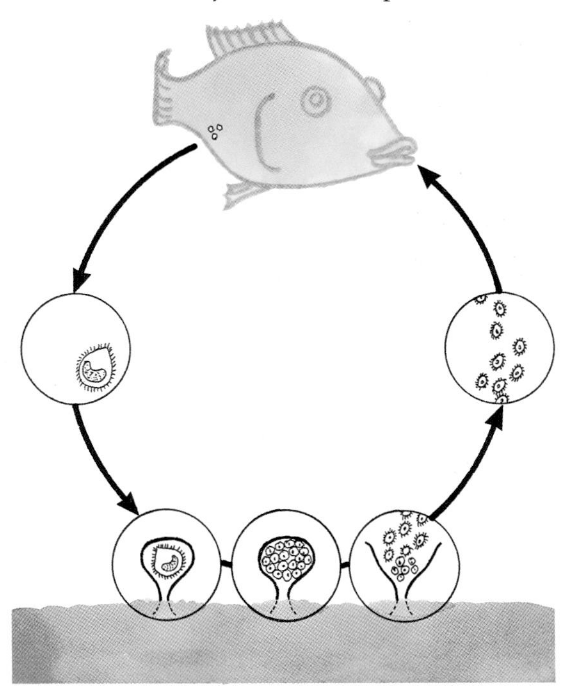

The single-celled parasites lodge under the skin of the host, breaking free when mature and encysting on the bottom. Each cyst attaches to the substrate while cell division produces more than 1,000 new, infective, parasites within. The cyst ruptures, releasing these to seek out a host. Only this infective stage can be treated effectively.

"White spot" or "Ich" is caused by the parasite *Ichthyophthirius multifiliis*, and is probably the most common disease of aquarium fishes.

***Melanotaenia* species (rainbow fishes) with a bacterial infection (*Myxobolus*).**

Other Crises

Euthanasia

Sooner or later you will need to destroy a fish which can no longer function properly as a result of illness or old age. The quickest and most humane method is to sever the spinal cord by cutting down hard just behind the head using a sharp knife. If you can't face the task, consult your vet.

Equipment Failure

Keep spares of items which go wrong commonly and suddenly, for example heater, air pump diaphragm. In the event of major failures – tank breakage, filter breakdown – at unsociable hours, seek help from the fishkeeping friends you should have made (including your dealer).

Power Cuts

Notify the electricity company of the loss of supply and get an estimate of duration. Keep tanks warm with blankets/quilts; plastic lemonade bottles, filled from the hot water tank, can be used as heaters. Use a battery-operated air pump or improvise aeration, for example hourly short sessions with a bicycle pump. Filter bacteria may be affected, so reduce/stop feeding and monitor ammonia/nitrite for a few days.

Going on Holiday

Properly maintained set-ups need no special preparation. Ask someone to check the fishes daily – ideally an aquarist, but if not leave the phone number of a "trouble-shooter" in case of any problems with the fishes or equipment. Most fishes will survive a fortnight without food and probably be healthier for it, but if you must have them fed, never leave a container of food – other people are invariably over-generous – but instead provide individually wrapped daily rations.

Breeding

Many aquarists soon develop a yearning for the patter of tiny fins, perhaps because a species breeds unprompted in its community tank, perhaps because of an interest in conservation. Indeed anyone maintaining a rare or endangered species should feel duty bound to try to breed it in order to reduce depletion of wild stocks. Legislation is currently being discussed which may forbid the importation of many (perhaps all) fishes from the wild, so the continued presence of many species in our aquaria may depend on captive breeding. You too may have an important role to play, rather than just breeding fishes for interest and amusement.

Unfortunately far too much breeding is unplanned and/or ill-considered, resulting in inferior stock. Many species which have been captive-bred for generations are now mere shadows of their splendid wild ancestors. They are also often unhealthy as lack of selection has reduced inherited vigour. A comparison of today's stock with photographs taken of the same species 20 or 30 years ago can be horrifying.

Breeding top-quality fishes depends on three factors: selection of parent stock; avoiding indiscriminate inbreeding; and rigorous culling of inferior offspring. Fishes intended for breeding should be vigorous, of good size and colour, with no inherited flaws in form and finnage – *never* the little chap you felt sorry for because he was the smallest, or the one with the funny twisted tail. Ideally they

Above: **Deformed fishes should never be used for breeding, and deformed fry culled at an early stage.**

Right: **A pair of *Hemichromis guttatus* (jewel cichlids) spawning.**

should be unrelated, although line-breeding (the planned mating of related individuals with a particular objective, usually the breeding of "fancy" strains of fishes, for example guppies) is acceptable. Rear only the best of the brood, even if there is a ready market – always cull deformed and undersized specimens (runts). The normal practice is to feed rejects to other fishes but if you are too soft-hearted, an aquarist friend will probably have a hungry predator.

Right: An *Oreochromis mossambicus* (Mozambique mouthbrooder) female taking her babies into her mouth to protect them from danger.

Below: Male anabantids such as *Betta splendens* (Siamese fighter) build bubblenests for the eggs, which they, rather than the females, subsequently guard.

A male *Barbus tetrazona* (tiger barb) (*right*) courting a female.

Most fishes do not actively care for their eggs, relying on sheer numbers to ensure the survival of a few – but in the restricted space of an aquarium all tend to become caviar for tankmates. Some species produce live young – which likewise usually become snacks. Some fishes, however, notably cichlids, actively care for both eggs and fry, their attendant territoriality often being to the detriment of anything sharing their aquarium. The courtship of some types can be equally traumatic for tankmates. For these reasons any serious attempt at breeding will usually require intervention by the aquarist, and frequently separate quarters for the breeding individuals.

The Breeding Tank

Natural requirements for water chemistry and habitat may have been compromised in the community tank, but the breeding tank should provide optimal conditions for its occupants, because without the correct water chemistry eggs often fail to hatch. Some species are seasonal breeders, requiring one or more triggers to stimulate spawning – in effect a simulation of what happens in Nature: the rains come (frequent water changes), food supply and quality improves (lots of live food), and then it gets hotter (raise temperature). Species from cool and temperate zones may also be triggered by longer day length (increased light intensity and duration). Some fishes require a particular spawning substrate (the surface on which, or material in which, eggs are laid). These special conditions are best created in a separate breeding tank, which must, however, in other respects conform to normal criteria for setting up and maturing aquaria for the species concerned.

The key to successful breeding is PATIENCE. Do not expect your fishes to breed the moment they are installed in their desirable residence – a change of environment is often the fishy equivalent of a cold shower! If nothing happens after a few weeks resist the temptation to fiddle with the environment (triggers apart); the fishes will probably have only just settled down enough to consider breeding, and your interference will set them back to square one.

Rearing

Mating and post-mating procedure varies for different types of fishes but there are general principles for fry rearing, whatever the species. First, fry are more delicate than their parents. They tend to be more susceptible to poisoning by nitrogen cycle by-products, so particular attention must be paid to water quality. Filtration turnover must, however, be gentle, as otherwise fry may be sucked in; small air-operated sponge filters are ideal. Zeolite, a material which absorbs ammonia, can be useful – a small amount scattered on the bottom of the tank, or suspended in a nylon bag (made from a stocking), will compensate for any hiccup in the filtration. Small fluctuations in temperature and water chemistry can have dire effects, so water changes, which should be small and frequent, require extra care.

Avoid moving tiny fry if possible – this often causes losses and/or a check in growth. Never use a siphon to move fry; this will cause physical damage. Instead use a meat baster or small soup ladle (extremely useful items when rearing fry) to transfer tiny fry; and for larger ones a small fine-meshed net designed for the purpose and available from your local dealer.

Above: A male *Gasterosteus aculeatus* (3-spined stickleback) with a week-old baby.

Below: *Pterophyllum scalare* (angelfish) with eggs on a leaf.

Types of Breeding Tanks

The illustrations below show some of the different techniques that the fishkeeper can adopt to help his or her fishes to breed in a safe and efficient manner.

1 Some fishes, for example small barbs, commonly eat their eggs. Reduce the level of water in the tank and place a layer or two of marbles along the tank bottom. The reduced water level means a shorter time that the eggs are in danger while they fall to the bottom of the tank, and the marbles act as a highly efficient fish-proof egg trap. Once spawning is over, remove all the eggs.

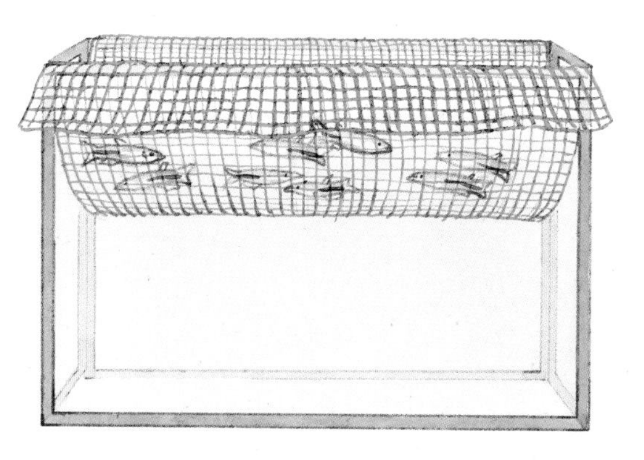

2 Another way of saving eggs is to drape a piece of finely meshed netting in the water. The fishes are placed above the netting, and when they spawn the eggs fall through it to safety. This method is suitable for small fishes such as danios.

3 A dense section of plants is required for breeding tetras. The fishes make spawning runs through the plants; their eggs are adhesive and remain trapped in the plants, safely hidden from other predators, to hatch.

4 Rainbowfishes can be successfully bred by the use of artificial mops. These are placed just inside the tank and provide a safe environment for the female fish to lay her eggs. It is then a simple job to collect up the eggs and hatch them in separate shallow dishes. Spawning mops are also used for breeding some killifishes (egg-laying cyprinodonts).

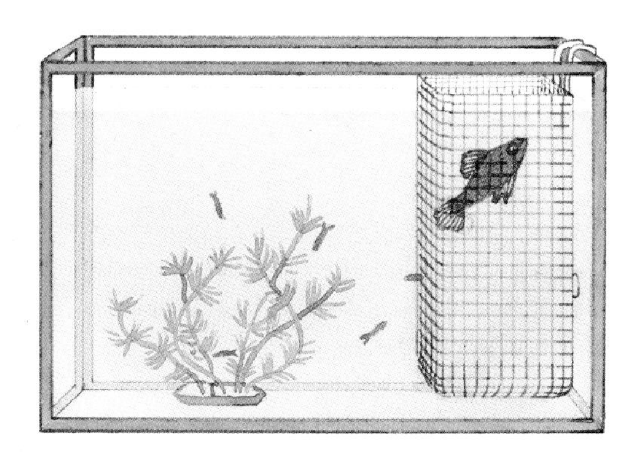

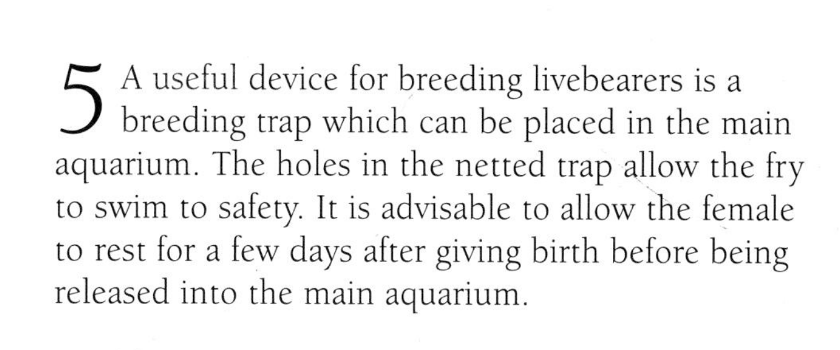

5 A useful device for breeding livebearers is a breeding trap which can be placed in the main aquarium. The holes in the netted trap allow the fry to swim to safety. It is advisable to allow the female to rest for a few days after giving birth before being released into the main aquarium.

Feeding Fry

Fish eggs, if viable, hatch after one or more days, but the larvae obtain nourishment from their yolk-sacs for several more days thereafter. They cannot swim at this stage and normally lie on the bottom or remain attached to the spawning substrate. When all the yolk has been absorbed they become free-swimming fry and start to look for food. Although they will find some natural foods (micro-organisms, algae) if the tank has been set up for some time, they usually need supplementary feeding immediately.

The type of food offered initially depends on the size of the fry; the tiniest will need infusorians: microscopic aquatic organisms which can be cultured by putting a lettuce leaf in a jam-jar, adding boiling water, and leaving the jar on a sunny window-ledge. When the water goes cloudy it is ready for use, and a portion can be drawn off with the meat baster and squirted into the shoal of fry. If the culture fails, there is a commercial substitute called "Liquifry" available.

The next size up of food, suitable for many newly free-swimming fry, is the freshly-hatched nauplii of the brine shrimp (*Artemia salina*), whose eggs (available from retailers) are hatched in salt water in lemonade bottles or large sweet jars.

***Loricaria* species (whiptail catfish) with eggs.**

The salt concentration depends on the geographical origin of the shrimps, so buy a brand with instructions. Start a culture two to three days before the fry are due to become free-swimming; once active, this will last for two to three days, so three, started at two-day intervals (and replenished on their sixth day), should suffice. Brine shrimp should always be rinsed in fresh water before feeding, to remove excess salt.

***Below left:* Male livebearers such as guppies and swordtails have a modified anal fin, the gonopodium, to permit internal fertilization of the females. *Below right:* Female *Xiphophorus* (swordtail) giving birth.**

Breeding coral fishes presents almost insuperable problems, though some success has been achieved with damsel and clown fishes. Feeding the fry remains a major hurdle to be overcome.

Another excellent fry food is microworm, cultured in plastic tubs of cold porage (or similar); the worms proliferate rapidly and crawl up the sides of the container away from the culture medium, and are harvested on a fingertip which is then rinsed in the tank. Starter cultures, with instructions, are often advertised in the aquatic press; thereafter a spoonful of established culture can be used to start others – after about 10 days the aroma tends to become unpleasant.

As fry increase in size they can take increasingly larger items – tiny pond foods such as *Cyclops*, *Bosmina*, and small *Daphnia*; cod roe; crumbled flake; and small particles of other foods. You will need to raise the young fishes to at least 2.5 cm (1 inch) long before they can be sold; good water quality and ample space are just as essential to growth as diet, so raise only as many as you can sensibly cope with, and regularly cull substandard individuals. The wise breeder canvasses potential customers (friends, dealers) early on (perhaps even before breeding a species at all) to find out how many fry it is worth raising; even if you could sell the entire brood, remember it is preferable to raise a small number of top-quality fry rather than a large number of poor ones.

Bibliography

Note: Some of the publications listed below are now out of print but we have included them because they are still available through public libraries.

Amlacher, E., *A Textbook of Fish Diseases*. T.F.H. Publications, Neptune City, New Jersey, U.S.A. 1970.

Andrews, C., *Fish Breeding*. Salamander Books Limited, London, U.K.. 1986.

Andrews, C., Excell, A. and N. Carrington, *The Manual of Fish Health*. Salamander Books Limited, London, U.K.. 1988.

Axelrod, A. assisted by S.R. Shaw, *Breeding Aquarium Fishes*. T.F.H. Publications, Neptune City, New Jersey, U.S.A. 1967.

Boyd, K.W., *The Complete Aquarium Problem Solver!* Tetra Press, Melle, Germany. 1990.

Dakin, N., *The Book of the Marine Aquarium*. Salamander Books Limited, London, U.K.. 1992.

Jocher, W., *Food for the Aquarium and Vivarium*. Studio Vista Limited, London, U.K.. 1966.

Kabata, K., *Diseases of Fishes. Book 1: Crustacea as Enemies of Fishes*. T.F.H. Publications, Neptune City, New Jersey, U.S.A. 1970.

Konings, A., (Ed.) *Enjoying Cichlids*. Cichlid Press, St Leon-Rot, Germany. 1993.

Konings, A., *Cichlids and all Other Fishes of Lake Malawi*. T.F.H. Publications, Neptune City, New Jersey, U.S.A. 1990

Konings, A., *Malawi Cichlids in Their Natural Habitat*. Cichlid Press, St Leon-Rot, Germany. 1995.

Mühlberg, H., *The Complete Guide to Water Plants*. E.P. Publishing Limited. 1980.

Rataj, K. and T.J. Horeman, *Aquarium Plants*. T.F.H. Publications, Neptune City, New Jersey, U.S.A. 1977.

Wickler, W., *Breeding Behaviour of Aquarium Fishes*. T.F.H Publications, Neptune City, New Jersey, U.S.A. 1973.

Zupanc, G.K.H., *Fish and Their Behaviour*. Tetra Press, Melle, Germany. 1985.

Table of Weights and Measures

1000 cubic centimetres = 1 litre
1 litre of water weighs 1 kilogram
1 cubic foot of water = 6.23 imperial gallons
1 imperial gallon of water weighs 10 lb
1 US gallon = .8 imperial gallon (approx)
1 imperial gallon = 4.55 litres

Glossary

Acidity/Alkalinity: the measure of the number of hydrogen ions in water, expressed in terms of pH. Neutral is pH 7, above pH7 is alkaline and below pH 7 is acid (*see also pH*).
Aeration: the movement of water created by a supply of compressed air into the aquarium.
Algae: simple aquatic plants, from tiny, single-celled, types to large seaweeds.
Biotope: any area that supports its own distinct community.
Bottom-sifter: a fish that eats by sifting through the substrate.
Brackish water fishes: fishes from water containing a measure of salt, but not as saline as seawater, such as river estuaries.
Brood: all the offspring of one family.
Bubblenest: a nest of bubbles which harbours the eggs of some fishes.
Carnivore: meat-eater.
Cold water fishes: fishes needing no heating of their water.
dH (of water): measurement of the amount of dissolved salts in water.
Diurnal (of feeding): feeding during the day (*see also nocturnal*).
Egg-layer: fishes that lay eggs which are then fertilized and hatched outside the female's body.
Epigean: living on or close to the surface of the water.
Filtration: the system for keeping the aquarium water clean.
Fresh water fishes: fishes from water containing no salt.
Fry: the young of a fish.
Genus: a group of closely related species.
Habitat: the physical environment of any individual species.
Hardness (of water): (*see dh of water*).
Herbivore: plant-eater.
Ichthyologist: person who studies fish.
Infusoria: tiny organisms which can be used as food for fry.

Barbus callipterus (clipper barb) is a West African barb. Growing to 9 cm (3 1/2 in) it is an undemanding species recommended for beginners. Ensure the tank is tightly covered as these fishes like to jump.

Insectivore: insect-eater.
Lacustrine: living close to the shore of a lake.
Livebearer: fishes whose fertile eggs develop inside the female's body.
Marine fishes: fishes that live in seawater.
Milt: fertilizing fluid of a male fish.
Mineral salts (in water): inorganic substances found naturally in water.
Mouthbrooder: fishes who hold their eggs and young in the oral cavity, during incubation, and also after the young are able to swim if danger approaches.
Mulm: accumulated fish waste, debris, unprocessed food, etc.
Nocturnal (of feeding): feeding at night (*see also diurnal*).
Ovipositor: a thin tube on the female's body used for planting eggs on surfaces, ready for fertilization by the male.
Parasite: a plant or animal that lives in or on another, gaining nourishment.
pH (of water): a logarithmic scale which describes acidity/alkalinity in water (*see also acidity/alkalinity*).
Piscivore: fish-eater.
Plankton: tiny organisms living on the surface of the water.
Salinity (of water): the amount of mineral salts present in seawater.
Specific gravity: the ratio of the density of a substance to that of water.

There are many fishes, such as this *Brachyplatystoma juruense*, that are just too large for the average home aquarium.

Acknowledgements

Picture Acknowledgements

The Publishers gratefully acknowledge the following photographers for permission to reproduce their work in this book.

Key: A: Above, B: Bottom, C: Centre, L: Left, R: Right, T: Top.

Mary Bailey: 3, 12 (2nd from T), 12 (T), 13 (B), 21, 39 (B), 43 (B), 63, 75 (B), 83 (T), 107 (B), 113 (B), 115, 118.

Bruce Coleman Picture Library: Jane Burton: 1, 2, 4, 7, 9, 10 (T, C), 11, 14, (T, L), 15, 16, 17, 18, 20, 25, 26, 34, 37, 38 (T), 39 (T), 45, 49 (T), 51, 53, 55, 56 (T), 57, 59 (B), 65, 69, 71, 72, 73, 75 (C), 76, 77, 81 (B), 85 (L), 86 (L), 88, 89, 90, 97, 100, 102, 103, 105, 109, 112, 114 (TR), 119, 120, 121, 122, 124 (BL, BR). **Hans Reinhard:** 44, 50, 67, 78, 116 (B)

Mike Sandford: 8, 10 (B), 12 (2nd from B, B), 13 (T),14 (R), 16, 19 (R), 22 (T), 23, 35, 36, 38 (B), 40, 42 (TL, BL), 46 (B), 54, 58 (B), 61 (T, L, R), 64, 66, 68 (B), 70 (B), 83 (B), 87, 96, 99, 100, 113 (T, C), 114 (TL), 117, 124 (T), 125

Publisher's Acknowledgements

For supplying aquatic equipment and allowing the practical photography to be completed on their premises :

Morden Waterworld
Morden Hall Garden Centre
Morden Hall Road
Morden, Surrey SM4 5JG
Tel: 0181 646 1066

For suppyling text on Australian heating and lighting systems, and advice on the installation of electrical equipment in the aquarium, the Publishers would like to thank Mr Norm Halliwell, a regular contributor to *Practical Aquariums*.

Author Acknowledgements

The authors would like to thank the following for advice and assistance: Mike Sandford and Nick Fletcher, who cast a critical eye over both content and grammar; Dr Keith Banister for scientific and taxonomic advice: Jeff Challands who used his computer and expert knowledge to allow our otherwise incompatible computers to communicate by floppy disc, thus avoiding the need for much re-typing; and Ad Konings for educating two insular Brits on the subject of metric tank sizes.

Also both our households for their tolerance and understanding during the disruption to domestic bliss occasioned by the writing of this book; and Dorothy and John Baker for their help in looking after MB's horse.

Finally, our particular thanks to British Telecom for taking only a week to restore viable communication between us at a critical stage of the enterprise....

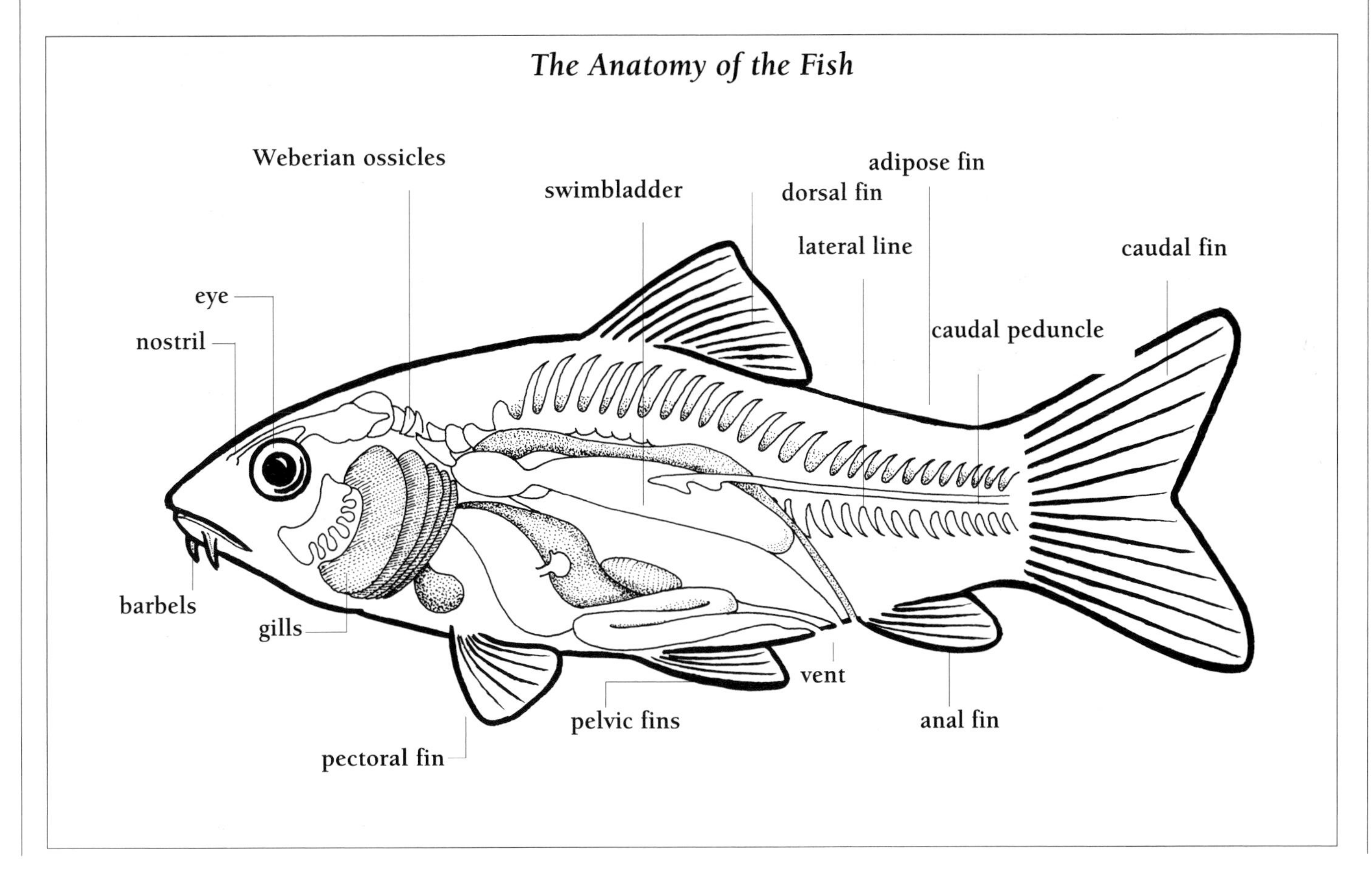

Index